Keto Diet Cookbook for Beginners:

2000 Days of Quick & Super Easy Low-Carb, Low-Sugar, High-Fat Recipes with a 30-Day Meal Plan for Effective Weight Loss and Optimal Health

Embrace a Healthy Lifestyle without Sacrificing Flavor

Emory Stout

Copyright © 2024 By Emory Stout. All rights reserved.

Legal Disclaimer & Image Notice

No part of this book may be copied, reproduced, or shared in any form without written permission from the publisher, unless it's for brief quotations used in reviews or articles.
The information in this book has been carefully gathered from trusted sources and is presented to the best of the author's knowledge and expertise. However, the author and publisher are not responsible for any mistakes, omissions, or damages that may result from using the content provided.

Medical Disclaimer

The recipes, nutritional details, and diet suggestions in this book are for informational and educational purposes only. They are not intended to replace medical advice, diagnosis, or treatment. Always consult a healthcare professional or doctor before making changes to your diet, especially if you have any pre-existing health conditions or dietary restrictions.

Image Disclaimer

The images in this book are meant for illustration only. The final look of the dishes may differ from the photographs due to variations in ingredients, cooking techniques, or presentation styles.
While we've made every effort to accurately depict the outcomes of the recipes, slight differences in appearance, texture, and color are normal. These variations are simply part of the cooking process and should not be seen as failures but as a result of individual preparation methods and ingredient availability.
The author and publisher are not responsible for any differences between the photos and the actual dish.

TABLE OF CONTENTS

INTRODUCTION..6
CHAPTER 1: KETO DIET BASICS...............7
    Welcome to the Keto Lifestyle.....................7
    Benefits of the Keto Lifestyle.......................7
    Understanding Ketosis................................8
    Essential Foods for Keto..............................9
    Managing the Keto Flu................................9
CHAPTER 2: 30-DAY MEAL PLAN...............10
CHAPTER 3: BREAKFASTS: Nutritious & Hearty Keto Breakfasts..14
    Spicy Ground Beef & Broccoli Stir-Fry.. 14
    Cheesy Zucchini & Herb Breakfast Casserole... 14
    Pesto Mushroom & Sundried Tomato Bacon Bake.. 15
    Garlic Steak Bites & Fried Eggs with Crispy Kale Chips.. 15
    Crispy Cauliflower Cakes with Garlic Aioli. 16
    Quick Keto Egg Muffins.......................... 16
    Savory Beef Hash with Butternut Squash and Bell Peppers.. 17
    Greek-Style Egg Bake with Feta, Spinach, and Kalamata Olives............... 17
CHAPTER 4: BREAKFASTS: Quick & Easy Keto Energizers..18
    Mushroom & Feta Stuffed Bell Peppers 18
    Beef Minced, Spinach & Cheddar Savory Waffle Sandwiches.................................. 18
    Turkey & Mozzarella Lettuce Wraps with Fresh Herbs.. 19
    Keto Egg Bowl with Ginger and Scallions. 19
    Zucchini Noodle Salad with Feta and Olives...20
    Keto Cheese Boats with Egg and Tomatoes... 20
    Cheesy Broccoli Waffles with Spicy.......21
    Yogurt Dip.. 21
    Egg Salad and Bacon Lettuce Cups..... 21
    Cheddar & Zucchini Herb Muffins with Thyme and Chives...................................22
    Vanilla Chia Seed Breakfast Pudding....22

CHAPTER 5: BREAKFASTS: Wholesome Keto Breakfast Innovations.................................23
    Avocado & Smoked Salmon Breakfast Boats.. 23
    Cheesy Broccoli & Ham Egg Cups........23
    Mushroom & Goat Cheese Breakfast Skillet... 24
    Coconut & Chia Keto Breakfast Pudding... 24
    Keto Berry Coconut Smoothie............... 25
    Creamy Avocado Matcha Smoothie...... 25
CHAPTER 6: BREAKFASTS: Keto Brunch for the Whole Family..26
    Family-Style Keto Breakfast Burrito Bowls 26
    Spinach and Mushroom Breakfast Lasagna..26
    Mushroom & Thyme Crustless Quiche..27
    Keto Hash Browns with Toppings.......... 27
    Almond Flour Crêpe with Ground Chicken and Vegetables...28
    Chicken and Spinach Breakfast Quiche 28
CHAPTER 7: LUNCHES: Delicious Keto Soups & Stews.. 29
    Slow-Cooked Lemon Herb Chicken & Kale Soup... 29
    Keto Broccoli Cheddar Soup with Crispy Prosciutto Crumble.................................. 29
    Rich Keto French Onion Soup with Caramelized Shallots and Gruyère........30
    Bacon Cheeseburger Soup.................... 30
    Mediterranean Eggplant & Tomato Stew with Fresh Basil and Olives...................... 31
    Slow-Cooked Chicken and Artichoke Stew with Spinach.................................... 31
    Roasted Cauliflower & Red Pepper Stew with Smoked Paprika.............................. 32
    Savory Mushroom & Sage Ground Turkey Stew..32
CHAPTER 8: LUNCHES: Unique Keto Bowls & Plates..33
    Burger Plate with Caesar Egg Sauce....33
    Beef & Broccoli Keto Stir-Fry with Sesame Oil and Vegetables................... 33

Mediterranean Roasted Vegetables with Turkey & Feta Power Bowl...................34
Greek-Inspired Stuffed Bell Pepper Halves..................34

CHAPTER 9: LUNCHES: Keto Pasta and Risotto............35
Pesto Shirataki Spagetti........................35
Meatball and Cheese Keto Rigatoni......35
Chicken and Spinach Creamy Risotto...36
Bacon and Broccoli Keto Risotto...........36

CHAPTER 10: LUNCHES: Gourmet Keto Meats......................37
Mediterranean Chicken & Vegetable Skewers with Tzatziki Sauce.................37
Grilled Chicken Breast with Lemon Butter Sauce...........37
Garlic Herb Lamb Chops with Cauliflower Mash and Fresh Thyme..................38
Keto Pork and Pistachio Meat Fingers.. 38
Tuscan Chicken Thighs with Spinach and Sun-Dried Tomatoes...................39
Beef Tenderloin with Creamed Spinach 39
Herbed Lamb Kofta with Mint Yogurt Sauce........................40
Keto BBQ Chicken Thighs with Apple Cabbage Slaw....................40
Ultimate Grilled Beef Burger with Aged Cheddar, Avocado & Caramelized Onions 41
Garlic Herb Butter-Crispy Chicken Drumsticks with Lemon Zest.................41
Herb-Crusted Pork Chops with Lemon Zest..................42
Grana Padano-Crusted Chicken with Zucchini.....................42

CHAPTER 11: SNACKS: Keto Light Treats... 43
Zesty Lemon Herb Chicken Wings........43
Jalapeño Poppers with Cream Cheese and Crispy Prosciutto.............................43
Eggplant Involtini with Ricotta and Basil 44
Crispy Halloumi Fries with Herb Dipping Sauce........................44
Cheesy Cauliflower Tots with Spicy Ranch Dip....................45
Creamy Spinach and Artichoke Dip Bites.. 45

CHAPTER 12: SNACKS: Keto Sauces & Spreads..................46
Creamy Avocado Cilantro Lime Dip......46
Keto Pesto Parmesan Dip.....................46
Spicy Avocado Jalapeño Cream Sauce 47
Garlic Parmesan Herb Dip....................47
Roasted Red Pepper and Feta Spread. 48
Cilantro Lime Yogurt Sauce..................48

CHAPTER 13: DESSERTS: Low-Carb Indulgences............49
Raspberry & Coconut Cream Parfaits with Chia Seeds..................49
Chocolate Almond Protein Bars...........49
Sugar-Free Walnut & Dark Chocolate Cream Cheese Truffles........................50
Spiced Berry Crumble "Bonfai Toffee" with Almond Flour Crust......................50
Keto Vanilla Bean Panna Cotta............51
Mocha Hazelnut Keto Bites..................51
Keto Tiramisu with Mascarpone Cream 52
Pumpkin Spice Cheesecake Bites.........52

CHAPTER 14: DESSERTS: Festive Keto Desserts..................53
Sugar-Free Lemon Tart........................53
Coconut Flour Brownies.......................53
Keto Strawberry Shortcake Cups..........54
Keto Espresso Chocolate Torte............54
Keto Almond Butter Cookies.................55
Elegant Keto Torte with Fresh Berries...55
Decadent Keto Chocolate Ganache Tart... 56
Creamy Coconut Lime Cheesecake......56
Lemon Ricotta Keto Pound Cake..........57
Matcha Green Tea Keto Cheesecake....57

CHAPTER 15: DINNER: Keto Dinners in Minutes..................58
Keto Broccoli Fritters with Cheese and Yogurt Sauce....................58
Keto Chicken Fajita Lettuce Wraps........58
Cheesy Zucchini Pizza Boats................59
Basil Pesto Chicken with Cherry Tomatoes....................59
Crispy Pork Chops with Cabbage Slaw. 60
Balsamic Steak Bites with Asparagus Spears.....................60
Keto Chicken Piccata with Zoodles.......61
Herbed Turkey Meatballs with Marinara

Sauce... 61
CHAPTER 16: DINNER: Filling Salads..........62
    Grilled Chicken Caesar Salad with Parmesan Crisps................................... 62
    Keto Nicoise Salad with Hard-Boiled Eggs 62
    Greek Salad with Grilled Lamb.............63
    Steak Salad with Spinach, Walnuts, and Balsamic... 63
    Crispy Chicken and Avocado Salad...... 64
    Bunless Steakhouse Salad....................64

CHAPTER 17: DINNER: Keto Vegan: Fresh Flavors...65
    Vegan Mushroom Stroganoff with Shirataki Noodles................................... 65
    Eggplant Caponata with Olives and Fresh Herbs... 65
    Cauliflower Steak with Herb Sauce........ 66
    One-Pan Keto Ratatouille with Bacon... 66

CHAPTER 18: DINNER: Taste of the Sea...... 67
    Spanish-Inspired Seafood Medley with Saffron Cauliflower Rice........................ 67
    Mediterranean Baked Sardines with Olive Oil and Fennel Salad.............................. 67
    Grilled Mackerel with Caper & Lemon Dressing... 68
    Herb Butter Shrimp with Creamy Cauliflower Gruyère Mash..................... 68
    Baked Mackerel in Tomato Sauce with Asparagus... 69
    Pesto-Crusted Salmon with Red Cabbage and Kale Salad...................................... 69
    Baked Cod with Olive Tapenade & Roasted Cherry Tomatoes......................70
    Seared Tuna Steaks with Avocado Salsa.. 70

CHAPTER 19: DINNER: Family-Style Favorites 71
    Garlic Grana Padano Chicken Wings....71
    Braised Pork Shank with Cabbage and Berry Sauce...71
    Baked Pork Ribs with Green Beans and Zucchini.. 72
    Keto Beef Wellington with Baby Bella... 72
    Creamy Tuscan Turkey Skillet with Sun-Dried Tomatoes & Spinach............ 73
    Roasted Duck Breast with Garlic Herb Butter & Sautéed Green Beans............ 73

CHAPTER 20: BONUSES.............................74
    30-Day Meal Plans with Shopping Guides: Simplified Keto Planning Made Easy.......... 74
    Grocery Shopping List for 7-Day Meal Plan.. 74
    Grocery Shopping List for 8-14 Day Meal Plan... 75
    Grocery Shopping List for 15-21 Day Meal Plan...76
    Grocery Shopping List for 22-30 Day Meal Plan...77
    Your Feedback is Valuable!........................78

INTRODUCTION

Dear readers,

Emory Stout, a professional chef with a focus on keto cuisine, is excited to share his book, Keto Diet Cookbook for Beginners. With years of experience in the kitchen, Emory has honed the skill of creating meals that are both incredibly tasty and fully in line with the keto diet principles.

In this cookbook, Emory brings together his culinary expertise and passion for healthy cooking. Each recipe is designed to be simple to make, packed with nutrients, and tailored to help with weight loss and improving energy levels. Knowing how tough it can be to make the switch to a keto lifestyle, Emory provides straightforward, easy-to-follow solutions that make it all easier.

The book also features a 30-day meal plan to help beginners smoothly transition into the keto way of eating. It's more than just a collection of recipes—it's a practical guide that shows you how to adopt and enjoy this lifestyle long-term. Whether you're new to keto or looking to expand your recipe collection, Emory's cookbook has everything you need to succeed.

CHAPTER 1: KETO DIET BASICS

Welcome to the Keto Lifestyle

The ketogenic lifestyle is more than just a diet—it's a transformational approach to health, energy, and vitality. While weight loss often takes center stage, the true power of keto lies in its ability to support mental clarity, stabilize blood sugar, and boost overall metabolic health, all while enjoying delicious, satisfying meals.

At its core, the keto diet emphasizes high-fat, low-carbohydrate eating, encouraging the body to enter a metabolic state known as ketosis. In this state, fat becomes your primary energy source, replacing glucose. This switch not only accelerates fat burning but also promotes sustained energy levels, reduces cravings, and supports optimal brain function.

Whether you're completely new to keto or looking to refine your approach, this book is your ultimate guide. We'll break down the science behind ketosis, highlight its benefits, and teach you how to adopt and sustain this lifestyle with ease. From essential foods and shopping tips to expertly curated recipes, you'll gain all the tools you need to succeed in making keto a permanent part of your life.

As a chef with years of experience in ketogenic cooking, I've designed this book to help you create meals that are both nutritionally balanced and bursting with flavor. With these recipes and insights, you'll discover that keto isn't restrictive—it's liberating, transforming how you think about food and your body.

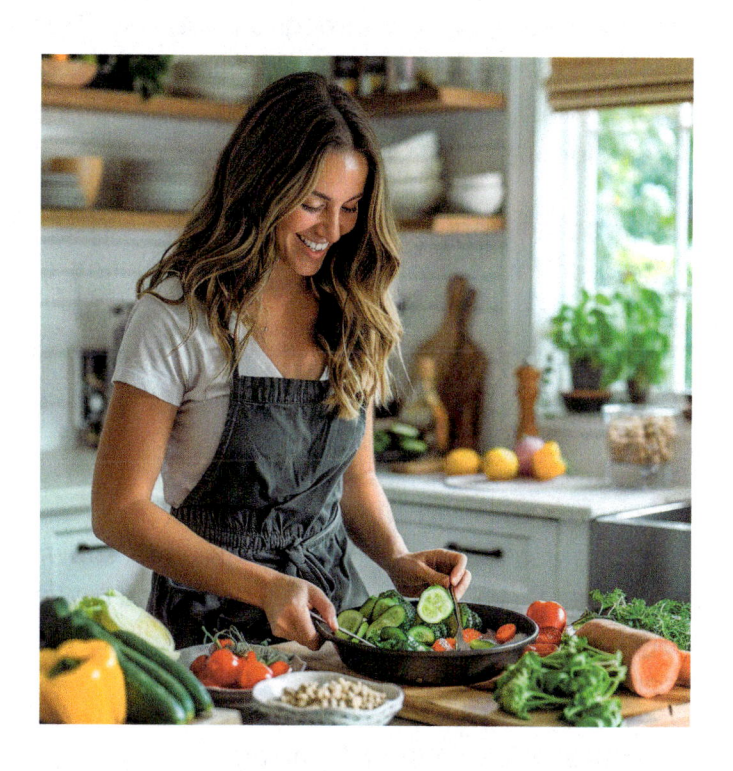

Benefits of the Keto Lifestyle

Adopting a keto lifestyle opens the door to numerous health benefits that go far beyond shedding pounds. Here's why keto has gained worldwide recognition:

1. Accelerated Fat Loss:
By reducing carb intake, your body transitions to burning fat for fuel, a process called lipolysis. This shift, coupled with lower insulin levels, encourages your body to tap into stored fat, leading to rapid and sustainable weight loss.

2. Enhanced Mental Clarity:
Ketones, the byproducts of fat metabolism, serve as a powerful fuel source for the brain. Many keto followers report improved focus, sharper memory, and a boost in cognitive function, making this diet particularly appealing to busy professionals and students.

3. Sustained Energy Levels:
Unlike the energy spikes and crashes associated with high-carb diets, keto provides a steady energy flow throughout the day. This stability is due to the body's reliance on fat, a more consistent and long-lasting fuel source than glucose.

4. Appetite Regulation:
The high-fat, moderate-protein composition of keto meals helps keep you fuller for longer, naturally reducing hunger and preventing overeating. This can lead to better portion control without the feeling of deprivation.

5. Improved Heart Health:
Despite its focus on fat, keto has been shown to increase HDL (good cholesterol) and lower triglycerides, contributing to better cardiovascular health.

6. Better Blood Sugar Control:
Keto helps stabilize blood sugar levels by minimizing carb intake. This makes it particularly beneficial for individuals with Type 2 diabetes or insulin resistance.

7. Reduced Inflammation:
A significant reduction in processed foods and sugars, along with an increase in anti-inflammatory fats, helps lower inflammation in the body. Many report relief from joint pain, clearer skin, and improved overall wellness.

8. Lifestyle Simplicity:
Once you're accustomed to keto, you'll find it offers plenty of delicious options. With countless recipes, meal prep becomes easier, and dining out is manageable with a few simple substitutions.

By committing to a ketogenic lifestyle, you're making a choice to prioritize your health in a way that is both enjoyable and sustainable.

Understanding Ketosis

What is Ketosis?
Ketosis is a metabolic state in which your body burns fat for fuel instead of carbohydrates. This shift happens when you drastically reduce your carb intake, forcing your body to rely on stored fat for energy.

How Does It Work?

1. **Fuel Shift:**
   Normally, the body uses glucose (from carbs) as its primary energy source. On keto, carb intake is reduced to 20-50 grams per day, depleting glycogen stores and prompting the body to switch to fat for fuel.
2. **Ketone Production:**
   The liver converts fatty acids into molecules called ketones, which serve as an alternative energy source for the brain, muscles, and other tissues.
3. **Efficient Fat Burning:**
   In ketosis, the body becomes highly efficient at breaking down fat for energy. This includes both dietary fat and stored fat, leading to weight loss and improved energy levels.

Signs You're in Ketosis:

- Reduced hunger
- Increased mental clarity
- Stable energy levels
- Mild bad breath (caused by acetone, a type of ketone)

Maintaining Ketosis:
Consistency is key. Stick to high-fat, moderate-protein, and low-carb meals while avoiding hidden sugars and high-carb foods.

Essential Foods for Keto

Healthy Fats:

- Avocados and avocado oil
- Coconut oil and MCT oil
- Grass-fed butter and ghee
- Olive oil

Proteins:

- Grass-fed beef, pork, and lamb
- Free-range poultry
- Fatty fish like salmon, mackerel, and sardines
- Eggs

Low-Carb Vegetables:

- Leafy greens: spinach, kale, arugula
- Cruciferous veggies: broccoli, cauliflower, Brussels sprouts
- Zucchini, bell peppers, asparagus

Keto-Friendly Fruits:

- Berries: strawberries, raspberries, blackberries
- Citrus: lemons and limes (used sparingly)

Dairy:

- Full-fat cheese
- Heavy cream
- Unsweetened almond or coconut milk

Foods to Avoid

To stay in ketosis, steer clear of:

- Sugary snacks and drinks
- Grains: bread, pasta, rice
- High-carb fruits like bananas and mangoes
- Starchy vegetables: potatoes, sweet potatoes
- Legumes: beans, lentils, chickpeas

Managing the Keto Flu

For beginners, the transition to ketosis can cause flu-like symptoms, known as "keto flu." Here's how to minimize discomfort:

1. **Replenish Electrolytes:**
   Increase sodium, potassium, and magnesium intake through foods like avocados, nuts, and leafy greens or by using supplements.
2. **Stay Hydrated:**
   Drink plenty of water to combat dehydration.
3. **Eat Enough Fats:**
   Ensure you're consuming enough healthy fats to fuel your body.
4. **Gradual Transition:**
   If symptoms persist, ease into the diet by gradually reducing carbs rather than eliminating them overnight.
5. **Rest and Recovery:**
   Allow your body time to adapt. Avoid intense workouts during the first few days and prioritize sleep.

By understanding the fundamentals of keto, choosing the right foods, and managing your transition effectively, you'll set yourself up for a successful and enjoyable ketogenic journey. This isn't just a diet; it's a lifestyle that transforms your relationship with food and your overall health

CHAPTER 2: 30-DAY MEAL PLAN

Day	Breakfast	Lunch	Snack & Desserts	Dinner
Day 1	Greek-Style Egg Bake with Feta, Spinach, and Kalamata Olives - p.17	Mediterranean Chicken & Vegetable Skewers with Tzatziki Sauce - p.37	Zesty Lemon Herb Chicken Wings - p.43	Spanish-Inspired Seafood Medley with Saffron Cauliflower Rice - p.67
Day 2	Pesto Mushroom & Sundried Tomato Bacon Bake - p.15	Slow-Cooked Lemon Herb Chicken & Kale Soup - p.29	Sugar-Free Walnut & Dark Chocolate Cream Cheese Truffles - p.50	Keto Chicken Piccata with Zoodles - p.61
Day 3	Quick Keto Egg Muffins - p.16	Bacon Cheeseburger Soup - p.30	Creamy Avocado Cilantro Lime Dip - p.46	Pesto-Crusted Salmon with Red Cabbage and Kale Salad - p.69
Day 4	Crispy Cauliflower Cakes with Garlic Aioli - p.16	Beef & Broccoli Keto Stir-Fry with Sesame Oil and Vegetables - p.33	Mocha Hazelnut Keto Bites - p.51	Herb Butter Shrimp with Creamy Cauliflower Gruyère Mash - p.68
Day 5	Savory Beef Hash with Butternut Squash and Bell Peppers - p.17	Mediterranean Roasted Vegetables with Turkey & Feta Power Bowl - p.34	Keto Tiramisu with Mascarpone Cream - p.52	Keto Beef Wellington with Baby Bella - p.72
Day 6	Mushroom & Goat Cheese Breakfast Skillet - p.24	Keto Broccoli Cheddar Soup with Crispy Prosciutto Crumble - p.29	Keto Pesto Parmesan Dip - p.46	Baked Cod with Olive Tapenade & Roasted Cherry Tomatoes - p.70
Day 7	Coconut & Chia Keto Breakfast Pudding - p.24	Mediterranean Eggplant & Tomato Stew with Fresh Basil and Olives - p.31	Spiced Berry Crumble "Bonfai Toffee" with Almond Flour Crust - p.50	Grilled Chicken Caesar Salad with Parmesan Crisps - p.62
Day 8	Cheesy Broccoli & Ham Egg Cups - p.23	Keto Chicken and Spinach Creamy Risotto - p.36	Keto Almond Butter Cookies - p.55	Grilled Mackerel with Caper & Lemon Dressing - p.68
Day 9	Avocado & Smoked Salmon Breakfast Boats - p.23	Bacon and Broccoli Keto Risotto - p.36	Spicy Avocado Jalapeño Cream Sauce - p.47	Keto Chicken Fajita Lettuce Wraps - p.58
Day 10	Cheddar & Zucchini Herb Muffins with Thyme and Chives - p.22	Keto Pork and Pistachio Meat Fingers - p.38	Keto Vanilla Bean Panna Cotta - p.51	Keto Nicoise Salad with Hard-Boiled Eggs - p.62
Day 11	Keto Egg Bowl with Ginger and Scallions - p.19	Slow-Cooked Chicken and Artichoke Stew with Spinach - p.31	Keto Pesto Parmesan Dip - p.46	Herb Butter Shrimp with Creamy Cauliflower Gruyère Mash - p.68
Day 12	Mushroom & Feta Stuffed Bell Peppers - p.18	Greek-Inspired Stuffed Bell Pepper Halves - p.34	Keto Chocolate Ganache Tart - p.56	Keto Beef Wellington with Baby Bella - p.72

Day	Breakfast	Lunch	Snack & Desserts	Dinner
Day 13	Vanilla Chia Seed Breakfast Pudding - p.22	Mediterranean Roasted Vegetables with Turkey & Feta Power Bowl - p.34	Keto Pesto Parmesan Dip - p.46	Grilled Mackerel with Caper & Lemon Dressing - p.68
Day 14	Beef Minced, Spinach & Cheddar Savory Waffle Sandwiches - p.18	Savory Mushroom & Sage Ground Turkey Stew - p.32	Creamy Spinach and Artichoke Dip Bites - p.45	Grilled Chicken Caesar Salad with Parmesan Crisps - p.62
Day 15	Keto Cheese Boats with Egg and Tomatoes - p.20	Bacon Cheeseburger Soup - p.30	Spiced Berry Crumble "Bonfire Toffee" with Almond Flour Crust - p.50	Pesto-Crusted Salmon with Red Cabbage and Kale Salad - p.69
Day 16	Keto Broccoli Waffles with Spicy Yogurt Dip - p.21	Keto BBQ Chicken Thighs with Apple Cabbage Slaw - p.40	Keto Tiramisu with Mascarpone Cream - p.52	Baked Cod with Olive Tapenade & Roasted Cherry Tomatoes - p.70
Day 17	Keto Egg Bowl with Ginger and Scallions - p.19	Mediterranean Eggplant & Tomato Stew with Fresh Basil and Olives - p.31	Creamy Avocado Cilantro Lime Dip - p.46	Spanish-Inspired Seafood Medley with Saffron Cauliflower Rice - p.67
Day 18	Cheesy Zucchini & Herb Breakfast Casserole - p.14	Roasted Cauliflower & Red Pepper Stew with Smoked Paprika - p.32	Keto Vanilla Bean Panna Cotta - p.51	Grilled Mackerel with Caper & Lemon Dressing - p.68
Day 19	Keto Berry Coconut Smoothie - p.25	Mediterranean Roasted Vegetables with Turkey & Feta Power Bowl - p.34	Spicy Avocado Jalapeño Cream Sauce - p.47	Herb Butter Shrimp with Creamy Cauliflower Gruyère Mash - p.68
Day 20	Cheesy Broccoli & Ham Egg Cups - p.23	Slow-Cooked Lemon Herb Chicken & Kale Soup - p.29	Mocha Hazelnut Keto Bites - p.51	Keto Beef Wellington with Baby Bella - p.72
Day 21	Coconut & Chia Keto Breakfast Pudding - p.24	Beef & Broccoli Keto Stir-Fry with Sesame Oil and Vegetables - p.33	Keto Almond Butter Cookies - p.55	Spanish-Inspired Seafood Medley with Saffron Cauliflower Rice - p.67
Day 22	Mushroom & Thyme Crustless Quiche - p.27	Greek Salad with Grilled Lamb - p.63	Creamy Spinach and Artichoke Dip Bites - p.45	Grilled Chicken Caesar Salad with Parmesan Crisps - p.62
Day 23	Cheddar & Zucchini Herb Muffins with Thyme and Chives - p.22	Keto Pork and Pistachio Meat Fingers - p.38	Keto Chocolate Ganache Tart - p.56	Keto Chicken Piccata with Zoodles - p.61
Day 24	Mushroom & Goat Cheese Breakfast Skillet - p.24	Beef & Broccoli Keto Stir-Fry with Sesame Oil and Vegetables - p.33	Keto Tiramisu with Mascarpone Cream - p.52	Baked Cod with Olive Tapenade & Roasted Cherry Tomatoes - p.70
Day 25	Cheddar & Zucchini Herb Muffins with Thyme and Chives - p.22	Bacon Cheeseburger Soup - p.30	Keto Pesto Parmesan Dip - p.46	Herb Butter Shrimp with Creamy Cauliflower Gruyère Mash - p.68

Day	Breakfast	Lunch	Snack & Desserts	Dinner
Day 26	Keto Egg Bowl with Ginger and Scallions - p.19	Mediterranean Roasted Vegetables with Turkey & Feta Power Bowl - p.34	Keto Pesto Parmesan Dip - p.46	Grilled Mackerel with Caper & Lemon Dressing - p.68
Day 27	Vanilla Chia Seed Breakfast Pudding - p.22	Keto Chicken and Spinach Creamy Risotto - p.36	Keto Almond Butter Cookies - p.55	Keto Beef Wellington with Baby Bella - p.72
Day 28	Cheesy Broccoli & Ham Egg Cups - p.23	Savory Mushroom & Sage Ground Turkey Stew - p.32	Keto Pesto Parmesan Dip - p.46	Grilled Chicken Caesar Salad with Parmesan Crisps - p.62
Day 29	Keto Egg Bowl with Ginger and Scallions - p.19	Mediterranean Roasted Vegetables with Turkey & Feta Power Bowl - p.34	Spicy Avocado Jalapeño Cream Sauce - p.47	Spanish-Inspired Seafood Medley with Saffron Cauliflower Rice - p.67
Day 30	Avocado & Smoked Salmon Breakfast Boats - p.23	Slow-Cooked Chicken and Artichoke Stew with Spinach - p.31	Keto Tiramisu with Mascarpone Cream - p.52	Grilled Mackerel with Caper & Lemon Dressing - p.68

Note: The 30-day meal plan in this book is a flexible guide to help you enjoy a balanced ketogenic diet. Caloric and macronutrient values are approximate and may vary based on ingredients and portion sizes. Adjust portions to suit your dietary needs and health goals. Use this plan as a starting point to explore delicious, nutrient-rich meals while personalizing your keto journey!

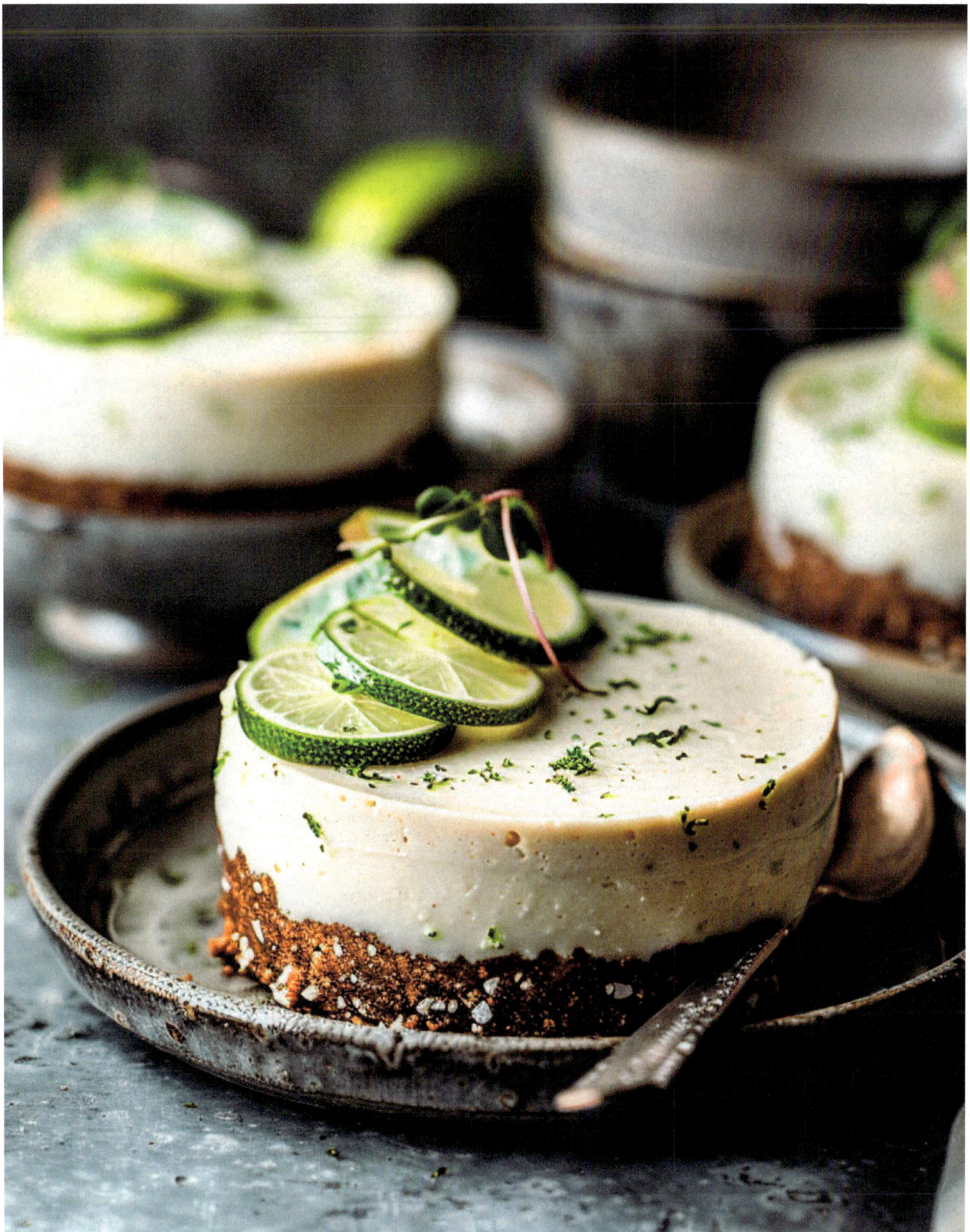

CHAPTER 3: BREAKFASTS: Nutritious & Hearty Keto Breakfasts

Spicy Ground Beef & Broccoli Stir-Fry

Prep: 10 minutes | Cook: 15 minutes | Serves: 2

Ingredients:

- 1 tbsp olive oil (15ml)
- 1 lb ground beef (450g)
- 2 cups broccoli, chopped (100g)
- 1/2 cup bell pepper, diced (75g)
- 1/4 cup onion, diced (30g)
- 1/2 tsp salt (2g)
- 1/4 tsp black pepper (1g)
- 1/2 tsp smoked paprika (1g)

Instructions:

1. Heat olive oil in a large skillet over medium-high heat.
2. Add ground beef, breaking it up with a spatula, and cook until browned.
3. Add broccoli, bell pepper, and onion, cooking until broccoli is tender, about 5 minutes.
4. Season with salt, black pepper, and smoked paprika. Stir well to combine and serve hot.

Nutritional Facts (Per Serving): Calories: 290 | Carbohydrates: 8g | Protein: 31g | Fat: 19g | Fiber: 3g | Sodium: 650mg | Sugars: 2g

Cheesy Zucchini & Herb Breakfast Casserole

Prep: 15 minutes | Cook: 15 minutes | Serves: 2

Ingredients:

- 1 tbsp olive oil (15ml)
- 2 cups zucchini, grated (100g)
- 1/2 cup cheddar cheese, shredded (75g)
- 1/4 cup heavy cream (60ml)
- 1/4 cup onion, diced (30g)
- 2 large eggs
- 1/2 tsp salt (2g)
- 1/4 tsp black pepper (1g)
- 1/2 tsp dried oregano (1g)

Instructions:

1. Preheat oven to 375°F (190°C) and grease a small baking dish with olive oil.
2. In a bowl, mix grated zucchini, cheddar cheese, heavy cream, onion, eggs, salt, black pepper, and oregano.
3. Pour the mixture into the baking dish and bake for 15 minutes, or until set and golden brown.
4. Let cool slightly before serving.

Nutritional Facts (Per Serving): Calories: 280 | Carbohydrates: 7g | Protein: 18g | Fat: 22g | Fiber: 2g | Sodium: 600mg | Sugars: 3g

Pesto Mushroom & Sundried Tomato Bacon Bake

Prep: 10 minutes | Cook: 25 minutes | Serves: 2

Ingredients:

- 1 tbsp olive oil (15ml)
- 1 cup mushrooms, sliced (90g)
- 1/4 cup unsweetened sundried tomatoes, chopped (40g)
- 6 strips bacon, chopped (120g)
- 1/4 cup pesto (60g)
- 1/4 tsp salt (1g)
- 1/4 tsp black pepper (1g)

Instructions:

1. Preheat oven to 400°F (200°C). Grease a baking dish with olive oil.
2. In a skillet over medium heat, cook bacon until crispy, then transfer to a paper towel to drain excess grease. In the same skillet, add mushrooms and sundried tomatoes, sautéing until softened and fragrant.
3. Transfer the mixture to the prepared baking dish, spreading it evenly. Drizzle pesto over the top and season with salt and pepper.
4. Bake for 15 minutes until the edges are golden, and the pesto is bubbling. Allow to cool for a couple of minutes before serving to let the flavors meld.

Nutritional Facts (Per Serving): Calories: 290 | Carbohydrates: 6g | Protein: 18g | Fat: 23g | Fiber: 3g | Sodium: 600mg | Sugars: 2g

Garlic Steak Bites & Fried Eggs with Crispy Kale Chips

Prep: 5 minutes | Cook: 20 minutes | Serves: 2

Ingredients:

- 1 tbsp olive oil (15ml)
- 10 oz ribeye steak, cubed (280g)
- 2 cups kale, torn (100g)
- 2 large eggs
- 1 tsp garlic powder (5g)
- 1/4 tsp salt (1g)
- 1/4 tsp black pepper (1g)

Instructions:

1. Preheat oven to 375°F (190°C). Spread kale on a baking sheet, drizzle with a bit of olive oil, and toss to coat evenly. Bake until crispy, about 10 minutes, tossing halfway. Remove and set aside.
2. Heat the remaining olive oil in a skillet over medium-high heat. Season steak bites with garlic powder, salt, and pepper, and sear until browned on all sides, about 3-5 minutes.
3. In the same skillet, reduce heat to medium and add eggs. Fry eggs to desired doneness, 2-3 minutes for sunny-side up or over-easy.
4. Serve steak bites and eggs alongside crispy kale chips. Garnish with additional pepper or a sprinkle of salt if desired, and enjoy hot.

Nutritional Facts (Per Serving): Calories: 300 | Carbohydrates: 5g | Protein: 32g | Fat: 20g | Fiber: 4g | Sodium: 650mg | Sugars: 1g

Crispy Cauliflower Cakes with Garlic Aioli

Prep: 10 minutes | Cook: 15 minutes | Serves: 2

Ingredients:

- 1 tbsp olive oil (15ml)
- 2 cups cauliflower, riced (100g)
- 1/2 cup almond flour (75g)
- 1/4 cup Parmesan cheese, grated (30g)
- 1 large egg
- 1/2 tsp salt (2g)
- 1/4 tsp black pepper (1g)
- 1/2 tsp smoked paprika (1g)
- For the Garlic Aioli:
- 1/4 cup mayonnaise (60g)
- 1 clove garlic, minced
- 1 tsp lemon juice (5ml)

Instructions:

1. Preheat oven to 375°F (190°C) and line a baking sheet with parchment paper.
2. In a bowl, mix riced cauliflower, almond flour, Parmesan, egg, salt, black pepper, and smoked paprika until well combined.
3. Shape the mixture into small patties and place them on the baking sheet.
4. Bake for 15 minutes, flipping halfway through, until golden brown and crispy.
5. Meanwhile, mix mayonnaise, minced garlic, and lemon juice in a small bowl to prepare the aioli.
6. Serve cauliflower cakes with garlic aioli on the side.

Nutritional Facts (Per Serving): Calories: 290 | Carbohydrates: 9g | Protein: 14g | Fat: 23g | Fiber: 3g | Sodium: 620mg | Sugars: 2g

Quick Keto Egg Muffins

Prep: 5 minutes | Cook: 15 minutes | Serves: 2

Ingredients:

- 6 large eggs
- 1/2 cup heavy cream (120ml)
- 1/2 cup cheddar cheese, shredded (50g)
- 1/2 cup diced bell peppers (75g)
- 1/2 cup spinach, chopped (30g)
- 1/2 tsp salt (2g)
- 1/4 tsp black pepper (1g)

Instructions:

1. Preheat oven to 375°F (190°C) and grease a muffin tin with non-stick spray or a little olive oil.
2. In a large mixing bowl, whisk together the eggs and heavy cream until smooth and well-blended. Season with a pinch of salt and pepper. Stir in the shredded cheddar cheese, diced bell peppers, and chopped spinach until everything is evenly distributed.
3. Pour the mixture into the muffin tin, filling each cup about 3/4 full to allow room for the muffins to rise. Bake in the preheated oven for 15 minutes or until the muffins are set, and the tops are golden brown. Remove from the oven and allow to cool for a couple of minutes before gently removing each muffin.

Nutritional Facts (Per Serving): Calories: 290 | Carbohydrates: 6g | Protein: 22g | Fat: 23g | Fiber: 1g | Sodium: 650mg | Sugars: 2g

Savory Beef Hash with Butternut Squash and Bell Peppers

Prep: 10 minutes | Cook: 20 minutes | Serves: 2

Ingredients:

- 1 tbsp olive oil (15ml)
- 1 lb ground beef (450g)
- 1/2 cup butternut squash, diced (65g)
- 1/2 cup bell peppers, diced (75g)
- 1/4 cup onion, diced (30g)
- 1/2 tsp smoked paprika (1g)
- 1/4 tsp salt (1g)
- 1/4 tsp black pepper (1g))

Instructions:

1. Heat the olive oil in a large skillet over medium heat. Add the ground beef, breaking it up with a spatula, and cook until browned, about 5-7 minutes. Drain any excess fat from the pan.
2. Add the diced butternut squash, bell peppers, and onion to the skillet with the browned beef. Stir well, ensuring the vegetables are coated in the beef juices and olive oil. Cook, stirring occasionally, until the butternut squash is tender and the peppers and onions are soft, about 10-12 minutes.
3. Season the mixture with smoked paprika, salt, and pepper. Taste and adjust seasoning. Serve the hash warm, garnished with fresh herbs.

Nutritional Facts (Per Serving): Calories: 300 | Carbohydrates: 8g | Protein: 30g | Fat: 20g | Fiber: 4g | Sodium: 650mg | Sugars: 2g

Greek-Style Egg Bake with Feta, Spinach, and Kalamata Olives

Prep: 10 minutes | Cook: 25 minutes | Serves: 2

Ingredients:

- 6 large eggs
- 1/2 cup heavy cream (120ml)
- 1/2 cup crumbled feta cheese (60g)
- 1 cup fresh spinach, chopped (30g)
- 1/4 cup Kalamata olives, sliced (40g)
- 1/4 tsp dried oregano (1g)
- 1/2 tsp salt (2g)
- 1/4 tsp black pepper (1g)

Instructions:

1. Preheat oven to 375°F (190°C) and grease a small baking dish with olive oil or non-stick spray.
2. In a mixing bowl, whisk together the eggs, heavy cream, salt, pepper, and dried oregano. Stir in the crumbled feta, chopped spinach, and sliced Kalamata olives.
3. Pour the egg mixture into the prepared baking dish, spreading it out evenly. Place the dish in the preheated oven and bake for 20-25 minutes, or until the center is set, and the edges are golden. Allow the egg bake to cool slightly before slicing. Serve warm, topped with a sprinkle of fresh oregano if desired.

Nutritional Facts (Per Serving): Calories: 290 | Carbohydrates: 6g | Protein: 22g | Fat: 23g | Fiber: 3g | Sodium: 700mg | Sugars: 2g

CHAPTER 4: BREAKFASTS: Quick & Easy Keto Energizers

Mushroom & Feta Stuffed Bell Peppers

Prep: 10 minutes | Cook: 25 minutes | Serves: 2

Ingredients:

- 1 tbsp olive oil (15ml)
- 2 medium bell peppers, halved and deseeded (150g)
- 1 cup mushrooms, diced (90g)
- 1/2 cup crumbled feta cheese (60g)
- 1/4 cup onion, diced (30g)
- 1/2 tsp dried oregano (1g)
- 1/4 tsp salt (1g)
- 1/4 tsp black pepper (1g)

Instructions:

1. Preheat oven to 375°F (190°C) and line a baking dish with parchment paper. Arrange pepper halves in the dish, cut side up.
2. In a mixing bowl, combine ricotta, spinach, Parmesan, basil, egg, salt, and pepper. Spoon the filling evenly into each pepper half.
3. Bake for 25 minutes or until the filling is set, and the tops are lightly golden. Allow to cool for a few minutes before serving.

Nutritional Facts (Per Serving): Calories: 290 | Carbohydrates: 9g | Protein: 14g | Fat: 23g | Fiber: 3g | Sodium: 620mg | Sugars: 3g

Beef Minced, Spinach & Cheddar Savory Waffle Sandwiches

Prep: 15 minutes | Cook: 15 minutes | Serves: 2

Ingredients:

- 200g ground beef (10% fat)
- 1 cup fresh spinach, chopped (50g)
- 1/2 cup shredded cheddar cheese (50g)
- 2 large eggs (100g)
- 1/4 cup almond flour (20g)
- 1/2 tsp garlic powder (2g)
- Salt and pepper to taste

Instructions:

1. Preheat a waffle iron and grease it lightly with olive oil. In a large skillet, cook the ground beef over medium heat about 5-7 minutes. Season with salt, pepper, and garlic powder. Set aside.
2. In a mixing bowl, whisk together eggs and almond flour, then fold in spinach and cheddar cheese. Add the cooked ground beef.
3. Pour the batter onto the preheated waffle iron, close, and cook until waffles are golden, about 5 minutes. Remove carefully and serve each waffle as a sandwich or open-faced.

Nutritional Facts (Per Serving): Calories: 340 | Carbohydrates: 3g | Protein: 39g | Fat: 33g | Fiber: 1g | Sodium: 650mg | Sugars: 1g

Turkey & Mozzarella Lettuce Wraps with Fresh Herbs

Prep: 10 minutes | Cook: 2 minutes | Serves: 2

Ingredients:

- 8 large lettuce leaves, washed (100g)
- 5 oz sliced turkey breast (150g)
- 1/3 cup shredded mozzarella (40g)
- 1/4 cup fresh basil, chopped (10g)
- 1/4 cup fresh parsley, chopped (10g)
- 1 1/2 tbsp Greek yogurt (20g)
- Salt and pepper to taste

Instructions:

1. Lay the lettuce leaves flat on a clean work surface. Pat the leaves dry with a paper towel if necessary.
2. Place sliced turkey breast on each pair of lettuce leaves. Sprinkle the shredded mozzarella cheese on top of the turkey. Sprinkle the chopped basil and parsley over the turkey and mozzarella.
3. Put greek yogurt onto each wrap. Season each wrap with a pinch of salt and pepper.
4. Roll up each lettuce wrap, folding in the sides as you go to keep the fillings enclosed. Secure with a toothpick if needed to prevent unrolling. Serve immediately for the best flavor and texture.

Nutritional Facts (Per Serving): Calories: 350 | Carbohydrates: 5g | Protein: 55g | Fat: 20g | Fiber: 2g | Sodium: 850mg | Sugars: 1g

Keto Egg Bowl with Ginger and Scallions

Prep: 10 minutes | Cook: 15 minutes | Serves: 2

Ingredients:

- 1 tsp sesame oil (5ml)
- 3 large eggs (150g)
- 1 1/2 cups shredded cabbage (90g)
- 2 tbsp shredded carrots (20g)
- 1/4 cup scallions, sliced (25g)
- 1 tbsp fresh ginger, minced (5g)
- 1 1/2 tsp soy sauce (7ml)
- Salt and pepper to taste

Instructions:

1. Heat sesame oil in a skillet over medium heat. Add the cabbage, carrots, and ginger, sautéing until the vegetables soften, about 5 minutes.
2. Whisk the eggs in a bowl, then pour into the skillet with the vegetables. Scramble gently until the eggs are cooked through.
3. Stir in soy sauce and scallions, and season with salt and pepper. Serve hot, garnished with extra scallions if desired.

Nutritional Facts (Per Serving): Calories: 305 | Carbohydrates: 11g | Protein: 21g | Fat: 20g | Fiber: 4g | Sodium: 650mg | Sugars: 5

Zucchini Noodle Salad with Feta and Olives

Prep: 15 minutes | Cook: 5 minutes | Serves: 2

Ingredients:

- 1 1/2 cups zucchini noodles (150g)
- 1/4 cup crumbled feta cheese (40g)
- 8 black olives, sliced (25g)
- 1 tbsp olive oil (15ml)
- 2 tsp lemon juice (10ml)
- 2 tbsp fresh basil, chopped (10g)
- Salt and black pepper to taste

Instructions:

1. In a large bowl, combine the zucchini noodles, crumbled feta, and sliced black olives.
2. Drizzle with olive oil and lemon juice. Sprinkle with fresh basil, salt, and black pepper.
3. Toss gently to combine. Let sit for 5 minutes to allow flavors to meld. Serve fresh.

Nutritional Facts (Per Serving): Calories: 332 | Carbohydrates: 10g | Protein: 10g | Fat: 29g | Fiber: 3g | Sodium: 1567 mg | Sugars: 3g

Keto Cheese Boats with Egg and Tomatoes

Prep: 5 minutes | Cook: 15 minutes | Serves: 2

Ingredients:

- 1/3 cup shredded mozzarella (40g)
- 3 large eggs (150g)
- 1/3 cup cherry tomatoes, halved (50g)
- 2 tsp olive oil (10ml)
- Salt and pepper to taste

Instructions:

1. Preheat oven to 375°F (190°C). Line a baking sheet with parchment paper to prevent sticking.
2. Divide the shredded mozzarella into two portions and form each into a "boat" shape on the baking sheet. Create a shallow well in the center of each cheese boat, making room for the eggs.
3. Carefully crack two eggs into each cheese boat. Distribute the halved cherry tomatoes around the edges. Drizzle with olive oil, and sprinkle with a pinch of salt and pepper.
4. Bake for 12-15 minutes, or until the egg whites are set, but the yolks remain slightly runny, and the cheese is melted and golden. Serve hot.

Nutritional Facts (Per Serving): Calories: 350 | Carbohydrates: 3g | Protein: 21g | Fat: 16g | Fiber: 0g | Sodium: 692mg | Sugars: 1g

Cheesy Broccoli Waffles with Spicy Yogurt Dip

Prep: 15 minutes | Cook: 10 minutes | Serves: 2

Ingredients:

- 1 cup finely chopped broccoli (100g)
- 1/2 cup shredded mozzarella (50g)
- 3 large eggs (150g)
- 1/4 cup almond flour (30g)
- 3 tbsp Greek yogurt (40g)
- 2 tsp olive oil (10ml)
- 1/2 tsp chili powder (2g)
- Salt and pepper to taste

Instructions:

1. Preheat a waffle iron and lightly grease with olive oil.
2. In a bowl, mix broccoli, mozzarella, eggs, almond flour, salt, and pepper until well combined.
3. Pour the batter into the waffle iron and cook for 4-5 minutes or until golden brown and crispy.
4. In a separate bowl, mix Greek yogurt with chili powder to create a spicy dip.
5. Serve waffles hot with the spicy yogurt dip.

Nutritional Facts (Per Serving): Calories: 378 | Carbohydrates: 4g | Protein: 37g | Fat: 25g | Fiber: 0g | Sodium: 567 mg | Sugars: 2g

Egg Salad and Bacon Lettuce Cups

Prep: 10 minutes | Cook: 2 minutes | Serves: 2

Ingredients:

- 4 large hard-boiled eggs, chopped (200g)
- 4 slices cooked bacon, crumbled (60g)
- 1/4 cup Greek yogurt (60g)
- 8 large lettuce leaves (100g)
- Salt and pepper to taste

Instructions:

1. In a medium mixing bowl, combine the chopped hard-boiled eggs and greek yogurt, stirring until the eggs are well-coated. Add the crumbled bacon and mix gently to incorporate. Season with salt and pepper to taste, adjusting to your preference.
2. Lay the lettuce leaves on a serving plate, arranging them to create little "cups." Spoon a generous portion of the egg salad mixture into each lettuce leaf, filling them evenly.
3. Carefully fold the lettuce around the egg salad to create a wrap-like shape, or leave open as cups for easy handheld eating. Serve chilled for a light, refreshing breakfast packed with protein and keto-friendly fats.

Nutritional Facts (Per Serving): Calories: 336 | Carbohydrates: 6g | Protein: 33g | Fat: 19g | Fiber: 1g | Sodium: 334mg | Sugars: 3g

Cheddar & Zucchini Herb Muffins with Thyme and Chives

Prep: 10 minutes | Cook: 20 minutes | Serves: 2

Ingredients:

- 1 cup shredded zucchini (130g)
- 1/2 cup shredded cheddar cheese (50g)
- 1/2 cup almond flour (60g)
- 2 large eggs (100g)
- 1/4 cup chopped fresh chives (10g)
- 1 tsp fresh thyme leaves (2g)
- 1/2 tsp baking powder (2g)
- Salt and pepper to taste

Instructions:

1. Preheat oven to 375°F (190°C) and line a muffin tin with 6 paper liners or grease with non-stick spray.
2. In a mixing bowl, whisk the eggs until smooth, then fold in shredded zucchini, cheddar, chives, and thyme. Add almond flour, baking powder, salt, and pepper, stirring until well combined.
3. Divide the mixture evenly among the muffin cups, filling each about 3/4 full. Bake for 20-22 minutes, or until the muffins are golden, and a toothpick inserted into the center comes out clean.
4. Let the muffins cool slightly in the tin before removing. Serve warm.

Nutritional Facts (Per Serving): Calories: 286 | Carbohydrates: 3g | Protein: 13g | Fat: 23g | Fiber: 1g | Sodium: 380mg | Sugars: 1g

Vanilla Chia Seed Breakfast Pudding

Prep: 5 minutes | Chill: 2 hours | Serves: 2

Ingredients:

- 3 tbsp chia seeds (30g)
- 3/4 cup unsweetened almond milk (200ml)
- 2 tbsp heavy cream (30ml)
- 1 tsp vanilla extract (5ml)
- 1 tbsp erythritol (10g)
- Pinch of salt

Instructions:

1. In a mixing bowl, combine the chia seeds, almond milk, heavy cream, vanilla extract, erythritol, and salt. Stir well.
2. Let the mixture sit for 5 minutes, then stir again to prevent clumping.
3. Cover and refrigerate for at least 2 hours (or overnight) until thickened.
4. Stir before serving and top with keto-friendly toppings if desired.

Nutritional Facts (Per Serving): Calories: 296 | Carbohydrates: 5g | Protein: 7g | Fat: 23g | Fiber: 11g | Sodium: 411mg | Sugars: 2g

CHAPTER 5: BREAKFASTS: Wholesome Keto Breakfast Innovations

Avocado & Smoked Salmon Breakfast Boats

Prep: 5 minutes | Cook: 2 minutes | Serves: 2

Ingredients:

- 1 small avocado, halved (120g)
- 2 oz smoked salmon (60g)
- 2 tbsp cream cheese (20g)
- 1 tsp lemon juice (5ml)
- 1 tsp olive oil (5ml)
- Salt and pepper to taste

Instructions:

1. Cut the avocado in half and remove the pit. Scoop out a small portion of flesh to make space for the filling.
2. In a bowl, mix cream cheese, lemon juice, and olive oil. Stir until smooth.
3. Fill each avocado half with the cream cheese mixture and top with smoked salmon.
4. Sprinkle with salt, pepper, and serve fresh.

Nutritional Facts (Per Serving): Calories: 330 | Carbohydrates: 7g | Protein: 13g | Fat: 29g | Fiber: 5g | Sodium: 910mg | Sugars: 1g

Cheesy Broccoli & Ham Egg Cups

Prep: 15 minutes | Cook: 20 minutes | Serves: 2

Ingredients:

- 1/2 cup chopped broccoli (80g)
- 2 oz diced ham (60g)
- 1/2 cup shredded cheddar cheese (50g)
- 2 large eggs (100g)
- 2 tbsp heavy cream (30g)
- 2 tsp olive oil (10ml)
- Salt and pepper to taste

Instructions:

1. Preheat oven to 375°F (190°C). Grease a muffin tin with olive oil or non-stick spray.
2. In a mixing bowl, whisk eggs with heavy cream, salt, and pepper. Stir in chopped broccoli, diced ham, and shredded cheddar.
3. Divide the mixture evenly among the muffin cups, filling each about 3/4 full.
4. Bake for 18-20 minutes, or until the egg cups are set and slightly golden on top.
5. Let cool slightly before serving.

Nutritional Facts (Per Serving): Calories: 286 | Carbohydrates: 1g | Protein: 25g | Fat: 19g | Fiber: 0g | Sodium: 284mg | Sugars: 1g

Mushroom & Goat Cheese Breakfast Skillet

Prep: 5 minutes | Cook: 15 minutes | Serves: 2

Ingredients:

- 1 cup sliced mushrooms (100g)
- 2 oz goat cheese (50g)
- 2 large eggs (100g)
- 1 tbsp olive oil (15ml)
- 1 tbsp heavy cream (20ml)
- 1 small garlic clove, minced (5g)
- Salt and pepper to taste

Instructions:

1. Heat olive oil in a skillet over medium heat. Add the mushrooms and cook for about 5 minutes until tender.
2. Stir in the minced garlic and cook for 1 more minute until fragrant.
3. Whisk the eggs with heavy cream, salt, and pepper. Pour over the mushrooms and cook, stirring occasionally, until eggs are set.
4. Crumble goat cheese on top, cover with a lid for 1 minute until slightly melted, and serve warm.

Nutritional Facts (Per Serving): Calories: 350 | Carbohydrates: 4g | Protein: 19g | Fat: 30g | Fiber: 1g | Sodium: 250mg | Sugars: 1g

Coconut & Chia Keto Breakfast Pudding

Prep: 5 minutes | Chill: 2 hours | Serves: 2

Ingredients:

- 3 tbsp chia seeds (30g)
- 3/4 cup unsweetened coconut milk (150ml)
- 2 tbsp heavy cream (30ml)
- 1 tsp vanilla extract (5ml)
- 1 tbsp erythritol (10g)
- Pinch of salt

Instructions:

1. In a mixing bowl, combine the chia seeds, coconut milk, heavy cream, vanilla extract, erythritol, and salt. Stir well.

Let the mixture sit for 5 minutes, then stir again to prevent clumping.

Cover and refrigerate for at least 2 hours (or overnight) until thickened.

Stir before serving and top with keto-friendly toppings if desired.

Nutritional Facts (Per Serving): Calories: 350 | Carbohydrates: 7g | Protein: 5g | Fat: 34g | Fiber: 5g | Sodium: 220mg | Sugars: 2g

Keto Berry Coconut Smoothie

Prep: 5 minutes | Cook: 2 minutes | Serves: 2

Ingredients:

- 3/4 cup unsweetened coconut milk (150ml)
- 1/4 cup mixed berries (strawberries, raspberries, blueberries) (40g)
- 1 tbsp chia seeds (10g)
- 1 tbsp MCT oil (10ml)
- 1/2 tsp vanilla extract (2.5ml)
- 1 tbsp erythritol (10g)
- Pinch of salt

Instructions:

1. Add all ingredients to a blender and blend until smooth.
2. Let the smoothie sit for 2 minutes to allow the chia seeds to expand slightly.
3. Pour into a glass and serve chilled.

Nutritional Facts (Per Serving): Calories: 350 | Carbohydrates: 7g | Protein: 4g | Fat: 33g | Fiber: 2g | Sodium: 210mg | Sugars: 2g

Creamy Avocado Matcha Smoothie

Prep: 5 minutes | Cook: 3 minutes | Serves: 2

Ingredients:

- 1/2 medium avocado (100g)
- 3/4 cup unsweetened almond milk (150ml)
- 2 tbsp heavy cream (30ml)
- 1 tbsp MCT oil (10ml)
- 1 tsp matcha powder (5g)
- 1 tbsp erythritol (10g)
- 1/2 tsp vanilla extract (2.5ml)
- Pinch of salt

Instructions:

1. Add all ingredients to a blender and blend until smooth.

Pour into a glass and serve chilled.

Nutritional Facts (Per Serving): Calories: 350 | Carbohydrates: 7g | Protein: 3g | Fat: 35g | Fiber: 4g | Sodium: 207mg | Sugars: 1.5g

CHAPTER 6: BREAKFASTS: Keto Brunch for the Whole Family

Family-Style Keto Breakfast Burrito Bowls

Prep: 10 minutes | **Cook:** 15 minutes | **Serves:** 2

Ingredients:
- 8 oz ground sausage or beef (225g)
- 4 large eggs, scrambled (200g)
- 1/2 cup shredded cheddar cheese (25g)
- 1/2 cup diced avocado (75g)
- 1/4 cup salsa (60ml)
- 2 tbsp sour cream (30g)
- 2 tbsp chopped fresh cilantro (8g)
- Salt and pepper to taste

Instructions:

1. In a large skillet over medium heat, cook the sausage or ground beef until browned and fully cooked, about 7-8 minutes. Drain any excess fat.
2. In a separate skillet, scramble the eggs with a pinch of salt and pepper until just set.
3. Divide the cooked meat, scrambled eggs, and toppings among four bowls. Sprinkle with cheddar cheese, add diced avocado, salsa, and a dollop of sour cream. Garnish with fresh cilantro. Allow to cool slightly before serving.

Nutritional Facts (Per Serving): Calories: 350 | Carbohydrates: 4g | Protein: 25g | Fat: 29g | Fiber: 2g | Sodium: 570mg | Sugars: 1g

Spinach and Mushroom Breakfast Lasagna

Prep: 15 minutes | **Cook:** 30 minutes | **Serves:** 2

Ingredients:
- 2 tsp olive oil (7ml)
- 1 cup fresh spinach, chopped (30g)
- 1/2 cup mushrooms, sliced (45g)
- 1/2 cup ricotta cheese (125g)
- 1/4 cup shredded mozzarella cheese (25g)
- 3 large eggs (150g)
- 2 tbsp heavy cream (30ml)
- Salt and pepper to taste

Instructions:

1. Preheat the oven to 375°F (190°C).
2. In a skillet, sauté the spinach and mushrooms in olive oil until softened, about 5 minutes.
3. In a mixing bowl, whisk together eggs, heavy cream, salt, and pepper. Layer the baking dish with half of the sautéed vegetables, followed by ricotta, mozzarella, and then pour half of the egg mixture. Repeat the layers and finish with mozzarella.
4. Bake for 25-30 minutes. Let it cool for 5 minutes before slicing and serving.

Nutritional Facts (Per Serving): Calories: 285 | Carbohydrates: 2g | Protein: 26g | Fat: 20g | Fiber: 0g | Sodium: 383mg | Sugars: 1g

Mushroom & Thyme Crustless Quiche

Prep: 10 minutes | Cook: 25 minutes | Serves: 2

Ingredients:

- 2 tsp olive oil (7ml)
- 2/3 cup mushrooms, sliced (60g)
- 3 large eggs (150g)
- 2 tbsp heavy cream (30ml)
- 1/4 cup shredded mozzarella cheese (30g)
- 2 tbsp grated Parmesan cheese (15g)
- 1/2 tsp fresh thyme leaves (2g)
- Salt and pepper to taste

Instructions:

1. Preheat the oven to 375°F (190°C). Grease a small baking dish with olive oil.
2. In a skillet, sauté the mushrooms in olive oil over medium heat until softened, about 5 minutes.
3. In a mixing bowl, whisk together the eggs, heavy cream, mozzarella, Parmesan, thyme, salt, and pepper. Stir in the sautéed mushrooms.
4. Pour the mixture into the prepared baking dish and bake for 20-25 minutes, or until the center is set.
5. Let it cool for 5 minutes before slicing and serving.

Nutritional Facts (Per Serving): Calories: 299 | Carbohydrates: 2g | Protein: 27g | Fat: 21g | Fiber: 0g | Sodium: 417mg | Sugars: 1g

Keto Hash Browns with Toppings

Prep: 10 minutes | Cook: 15 minutes | Serves: 2

Ingredients:

- 1 cup shredded cauliflower (100g)
- 1/4 cup shredded cheddar cheese (25g)
- 1 large egg (50g)
- 1/8 tsp garlic powder (0.5g)
- Salt and pepper to taste
- Toppings:
- 1/4 cup sour cream (60g)
- 1/4 cup diced avocado (38g)
- 2 tbsp cooked bacon crumbles (15g)
- Fresh chives for garnish

Instructions:

1. In a mixing bowl, combine cauliflower, cheddar cheese, egg, garlic powder, salt, and pepper. Stir until well combined.
2. Heat a non-stick skillet over medium heat with a small amount of oil. Form the mixture into small patties and cook in batches for 3-4 minutes per side, or until golden and crisp.
3. Serve the hash browns topped with sour cream, diced avocado, bacon crumbles, and a sprinkle of fresh chives. Enjoy hot for a keto-friendly breakfast with all the classic flavors.

Nutritional Facts (Per Serving): Calories: 298 | Carbohydrates: 4g | Protein: 14g | Fat: 26g | Fiber: 2g | Sodium: 360mg | Sugars: 1g

Almond Flour Crêpe with Ground Chicken and Vegetables

Prep: 15 minutes | Cook: 20 minutes | Serves: 2

Ingredients:

- 1/2 cup almond flour (50g)
- 1/2 cup water (120ml)
- 2 tbsp olive oil, divided (30ml)
- 1/2 lb ground chicken (225g)
- 1/2 cup bell pepper, diced (75g)
- 1/2 cup zucchini, diced (75g)
- 1/4 cup onion, diced (30g)
- Salt and pepper to taste

Instructions:

1. In a bowl, whisk together almond flour and water until smooth. Heat 1 tbsp olive oil in a non-stick skillet over medium heat, then pour in half of the batter, spreading it thinly to form a crêpe. Cook for 2-3 minutes per side until set. Repeat with the remaining batter to make two crêpes.
2. In a separate skillet, heat the remaining 1 tbsp olive oil over medium-high heat. Add ground chicken and cook until browned, about 5-7 minutes. Add bell pepper, zucchini, and onion, cooking until vegetables are tender. Season with salt and pepper.
3. Place half of the chicken and vegetable mixture on each crêpe, fold, and serve warm.

Nutritional Facts (Per Serving): Calories: 350 | Carbohydrates: 5g | Protein: 41g | Fat: 33g | Fiber: 4g | Sodium: 476mg | Sugars: 4g

Chicken and Spinach Breakfast Quiche

Prep: 10 minutes | Cook: 35 minutes | Serves: 2

Ingredients:

- 1/2 lb cooked shredded chicken (225g)
- 1 cup fresh spinach, chopped (30g)
- 6 large eggs (300g)
- 1/2 cup heavy cream (120ml)
- 1/2 cup shredded mozzarella cheese (50g)
- Salt and pepper to taste

Instructions:

1. Preheat the oven to 375°F (190°C) and grease a small baking dish or pie pan with a little oil.
2. Spread shredded chicken and chopped spinach evenly over the bottom of the dish.
3. In a bowl, whisk together eggs, heavy cream, salt, and pepper until smooth. Pour the mixture over the chicken and spinach, then sprinkle mozzarella on top.
4. Bake for 30-35 minutes, or until the quiche is set, and the top is golden. Allow to cool slightly before slicing and serving. This quiche is perfect for a satisfying, low-carb breakfast.

Nutritional Facts (Per Serving): Calories: 569 | Carbohydrates: 4g | Protein: 52g | Fat: 39g | Fiber: 0g | Sodium: 766mg | Sugars: 2g

CHAPTER 7: LUNCHES: Delicious Keto Soups & Stews

Slow-Cooked Lemon Herb Chicken & Kale Soup

Prep: 10 minutes | Cook: 4 hours | Serves: 2

Ingredients:

- 14 oz boneless, skinless chicken thighs (400g)
- 5 cups low-carb chicken broth (1200ml)
- 3 cups chopped kale (80g)
- 2 small zucchinis, sliced (300g)
- 1/2 cup chopped celery (50g)
- 2 tbsp olive oil (30ml)
- Juice of 1 lemon (30ml)
- 2 tsp fresh thyme (6g)
- 2 tsp fresh rosemary, chopped (6g)
- 1 tsp garlic powder (4g)
- Salt and pepper to taste

Instructions:

1. In a slow cooker, combine chicken, broth, kale, zucchini, and celery.
2. Add lemon juice, thyme, rosemary, garlic powder, and a pinch of salt and pepper.
3. Cover and cook on low for 4 hours, or until chicken is tender and vegetables are soft.
4. Shred the chicken in the pot, stir, and season to taste.

Nutritional Facts (Per Serving): Calories: 595 | Sugars: 1g | Fat: 46g | Carbohydrates: 8g | Protein: 44g | Fiber: 4g | Sodium: 650mg

Keto Broccoli Cheddar Soup with Crispy Prosciutto Crumble

Prep: 15 minutes | Cook: 20 minutes | Serves: 2

Ingredients:

- 5 cups broccoli florets (375g)
- 2 1/2 cups low-carb chicken broth (600ml)
- 1 1/4 cups heavy cream (300ml)
- 1 1/4 cups shredded cheddar cheese (125g)
- 3 slices prosciutto, crumbled
- 1/2 tsp garlic powder (2g)
- 1/2 tsp onion powder (2g)
- Salt and pepper to taste

Instructions:

1. In a large pot, bring broth to a boil and add broccoli. Cook until tender, about 10 minutes.
2. Add heavy cream, cheddar, garlic powder, and onion powder. Simmer until cheese melts and soup thickens.
3. In a skillet, crisp prosciutto over medium heat, crumble, and sprinkle over soup before serving.

Nutritional Facts (Per Serving): Calories: 590 | Sugars: 2g | Fat: 50g | Carbohydrates: 7g | Protein: 34g | Fiber: 4g | Sodium: 700mg

Rich Keto French Onion Soup with Caramelized Shallots and Gruyère

Prep: 10 minutes | Cook: 35 minutes | Serves: 2

Ingredients:

- 4 medium shallots, thinly sliced (160g)
- 4 tbsp butter (60g)
- 3 1/2 cups low-carb beef broth (840ml)
- 3/4 cup shredded Gruyère cheese (75g)
- 1 tbsp low-carb sweetener (optional)
- 1/2 tsp fresh thyme leaves (1g)
- Salt and pepper to taste

Instructions:

1. In a pot, melt butter over medium heat. Add the sliced shallots and cook, stirring occasionally, until golden brown and caramelized, about 15 minutes. Adjust heat as needed to prevent burning.
2. Add the beef broth, sweetener (if using), thyme, salt, and pepper. Stir to combine and bring to a simmer. Reduce the heat slightly and let it cook for another 15 minutes to blend the flavors.
3. Divide the soup between oven-safe bowls, sprinkle Gruyère cheese over each, and broil until the cheese is melted and bubbly, about 2-3 minutes. Watch closely to avoid over-browning.

Nutritional Facts (Per Serving): Calories: 595 | Sugars: 1g | Fat: 50g | Carbohydrates: 8g | Protein: 33g | Fiber: 4g | Sodium: 650mg

Bacon Cheeseburger Soup

Prep: 10 minutes | Cook: 25 minutes | Serves: 2

Ingredients:

- 2/3 lb ground beef (300g)
- 5 slices bacon, diced (75g)
- 2 1/2 cups low-carb beef broth (600ml)
- 1 1/4 cups shredded cheddar cheese (125g)
- 2/3 cup heavy cream (160ml)
- 1/2 cup diced celery (50g)
- 1/3 cup diced onion (40g)
- 1 tsp garlic powder (5g)
- Salt and pepper to taste

Instructions:

1. In a large pot over medium heat, cook diced bacon until crispy, about 5 minutes. Remove with a slotted spoon and set aside, leaving the rendered fat in the pot.
2. Add the ground beef to the pot and cook until browned, breaking it up as it cooks, about 5 minutes. Add the celery, onion, and garlic powder, stirring until vegetables are soft, about 3-4 minutes.
3. Pour in beef broth and heavy cream, stirring to combine. Gradually add cheddar cheese, stirring continuously to ensure it melts smoothly.
4. Add the crispy bacon back to the pot, stir, and season with salt and pepper to taste. Ladle into bowls and serve warm.

Nutritional Facts (Per Serving): Calories: 600 | Sugars: 1g | Fat: 52g | Carbohydrates: 7g | Protein: 38g | Fiber: 3g | Sodium: 680mg

Mediterranean Eggplant & Tomato Stew with Fresh Basil and Olives

Prep: 15 minutes | Cook: 30 minutes | Serves: 2

Ingredients:

- 1 large eggplant, diced (300g)
- 1 can low-sodium diced tomatoes (14 oz) (400g)
- 2/3 cup pitted Kalamata olives, sliced (100g)
- 1/3 cup chopped fresh basil (15g)
- 3 tbsp olive oil (45ml)
- 3/4 tsp smoked paprika (3g)
- Salt and pepper to taste

Instructions:

1. Heat olive oil in a large pot over medium heat. Add the diced eggplant, stirring occasionally to cook all sides evenly. Sauté the eggplant for about 8 minutes until it becomes soft and lightly golden.
2. Add the can of diced tomatoes, olives, smoked paprika, salt, and pepper. Stir to mix all ingredients, ensuring the eggplant is well-coated with tomatoes and seasonings.
3. Reduce the heat to low, cover the pot, and let the stew simmer for 20 minutes. Stir every 5 minutes to prevent sticking.
4. Once cooked, remove from heat, stir in fresh basil, and taste. Adjust seasonings if needed before serving. Serve warm with extra basil if desired.

Nutritional Facts (Per Serving): Calories: 590 | Sugars: 3g | Fat: 50g | Carbohydrates: 10g | Protein: 7g | Fiber: 6g | Sodium: 480mg

Slow-Cooked Chicken and Artichoke Stew with Spinach

Prep: 10 minutes | Cook: 4 hours | Serves: 2

Ingredients:

- 1.2 lb boneless chicken thighs, diced (550g)
- 1 1/4 cups artichoke hearts, halved (190g)
- 3 cups fresh spinach (90g)
- 3/4 cup low-sodium chicken broth (180ml)
- 1 1/2 tbsp lemon juice (22ml)
- 2 tbsp olive oil (30ml)
- Salt and pepper to taste

Instructions:

1. Place diced chicken thighs in the slow cooker. Add artichoke hearts, chicken broth, lemon juice, and olive oil. Season generously with salt and pepper, then stir.
2. Cover and cook on low for 4 hours, allowing the chicken to become tender and absorb the flavors of the artichokes and broth.
3. After 4 hours, add the spinach, stirring it into the stew until it begins to wilt. Cover and cook for an additional 10 minutes, letting the spinach fully incorporate into the stew.
4. Once cooked, taste and adjust seasonings if necessary. Serve warm, garnished with a sprinkle of fresh herbs or extra lemon juice if desired.

Nutritional Facts (Per Serving): Calories: 600 | Sugars: 1g | Fat: 50g | Carbohydrates: 6g | Protein: 45g | Fiber: 4g | Sodium: 580mg

Roasted Cauliflower & Red Pepper Stew with Smoked Paprika

Prep: 15 minutes | Cook: 30 minutes | Serves: 2

Ingredients:

- 2 1/2 cups cauliflower florets (250g)
- 1 large red bell pepper, diced (180g)
- 1 can low-sodium diced tomatoes (14 oz) (400g)
- 5 tbsp olive oil (75ml)
- 1 1/4 tsp smoked paprika (5g)
- Salt and pepper to taste

Instructions:

1. Preheat the oven to 400°F (200°C). Toss the cauliflower florets and diced red bell pepper with 2 tbsp of olive oil, a pinch of salt, and pepper. Spread them on a baking sheet in a single layer.
2. Roast the vegetables in the oven for 20 minutes, or until they are tender and lightly browned, turning halfway through cooking for even roasting.
3. In a large pot, heat the remaining 2 tbsp of olive oil over medium heat. Add the roasted cauliflower and red pepper, along with the diced tomatoes and smoked paprika. Stir well to combine.
4. Reduce the heat to low, cover, and let the stew simmer for 10 minutes. Taste and adjust seasonings as needed before serving. Serve hot.

Nutritional Facts (Per Serving): Calories: 590 | Sugars: 3g | Fat: 53g | Carbohydrates: 9g | Protein: 5g | Fiber: 6g | Sodium: 450mg

Savory Mushroom & Sage Ground Turkey Stew

Prep: 10 minutes | Cook: 25 minutes | Serves: 2

Ingredients:

- 2/3 lb ground turkey (300g)
- 1 1/4 cups sliced mushrooms (125g)
- 2 1/2 cups low-sodium chicken broth (600ml)
- 1 1/2 tbsp fresh sage, chopped (9g)
- 3 tbsp olive oil (45ml)
- Salt and pepper to taste

Instructions:

1. Heat 1 tbsp olive oil in a large pot over medium heat. Add the ground turkey and cook, breaking it into small pieces, about 8 minutes. Season with salt and pepper to taste.
2. Move the turkey to one side of the pot and add the remaining 1 tbsp olive oil. Add the sliced mushrooms and cook, stirring occasionally, until the mushrooms are soft and golden brown, about 5 minutes. Combine with the turkey in the pot.
3. Pour in the chicken broth and stir in the chopped sage. Bring the mixture to a gentle simmer and let it cook for 10-12 minutes.
4. Taste and adjust seasonings as desired before serving. Ladle into bowls and serve warm.

Nutritional Facts (Per Serving): Calories: 600 | Sugars: 1g | Fat: 50g | Carbohydrates: 7g | Protein: 42g | Fiber: 3g | Sodium: 550mg

CHAPTER 8: LUNCHES: Unique Keto Bowls & Plates

Burger Plate with Caesar Egg Sauce

Prep: 15 minutes | Cook: 15 minutes | Serves: 2

Ingredients:

- 4 large lettuce leaves
- 2/3 cucumber, sliced (130g)
- 3/4 lb beef or chicken skewers, grilled and cut into chunks (340g)
- 1/3 cup shredded hard cheese, such as Parmesan (40g)
- 5 slices crispy bacon (75g)

Caesar Egg Sauce:
- 2 large egg yolks
- 1 1/2 tsp Dijon mustard (7g)
- 3 tbsp olive oil (45ml)
- 1 1/2 tsp lemon juice (7ml)
- Salt and pepper to taste

Instructions:

1. Arrange lettuce leaves and cucumber slices on a plate. Scatter grilled meat chunks, shredded cheese, and bacon over the top.
2. To make the Caesar egg sauce, whisk egg yolk, mustard, lemon juice, salt, and pepper in a small bowl. Gradually whisk in olive oil until smooth and creamy.
3. Drizzle Caesar sauce over the plate and serve.

Nutritional Facts (Per Serving): Calories: 600 | Sugars: 1g | Fat: 50g | Carbohydrates: 7g | Protein: 45g | Fiber: 3g | Sodium: 550mg

Beef & Broccoli Keto Stir-Fry with Sesame Oil and Vegetables

Prep: 10 minutes | Cook: 20 minutes | Serves: 2

Ingredients:

- 3/4 lb beef strips (340g)
- 2 1/2 cups broccoli florets (190g)
- 2/3 cup sliced bell peppers (100g)
- 2/3 cup zucchini, sliced (100g)
- 1 1/2 tbsp sesame oil (22ml)
- 3 tbsp low-sodium soy sauce (45ml)
- 2 cloves garlic, minced
- Salt and pepper to taste

Instructions:

1. Heat the sesame oil in a large skillet over medium heat. Add the beef strips, seasoning with salt and pepper. Stir-fry the beef for about 5 minutes, turning occasionally.
2. Add the minced garlic and stir for 1 minute. Add the broccoli florets, bell peppers, and zucchini.
3. Pour in the soy sauce, stirring well. Continue cooking for another 7-10 minutes. Adjust the seasoning with additional salt and pepper. Serve warm.

Nutritional Facts (Per Serving): Calories: 590 | Sugars: 2g | Fat: 48g | Carbohydrates: 8g | Protein: 40g | Fiber: 4g | Sodium: 600mg

Mediterranean Roasted Vegetables with Turkey & Feta Power Bowl

Prep: 10 minutes | Cook: 25 minutes | Serves: 2

Ingredients:

- 3/4 lb ground turkey, cooked (340g)
- 1 large zucchini, sliced (200g)
- 1 red bell pepper, diced (130g)
- 1/2 red onion, sliced (60g)
- 1/3 cup crumbled feta cheese (40g)
- 3 tbsp olive oil (45ml)
- 1 1/2 tbsp fresh parsley, chopped (7g)
- Salt and pepper to taste

Instructions:

1. Preheat oven to 400°F (200°C). Toss zucchini, bell pepper, and onion with 1 tbsp olive oil, salt, and pepper. Spread on a baking sheet in a single layer and roast for 20 minutes, until tender and slightly browned.
2. While vegetables are roasting, heat the remaining 1 tbsp olive oil in a skillet over medium heat. Cook ground turkey, seasoning lightly with salt and pepper, until browned, about 6-8 minutes.
3. Assemble the bowls by layering the roasted vegetables and cooked turkey, topping with crumbled feta, and garnishing with fresh parsley. Serve warm.

Nutritional Facts (Per Serving): Calories: 600 | Sugars: 3g | Fat: 50g | Carbohydrates: 8g | Protein: 42g | Fiber: 5g | Sodium: 500mg

Greek-Inspired Stuffed Bell Pepper Halves

Prep: 15 minutes | Cook: 25 minutes | Serves: 2

Ingredients:

- 2 large bell peppers, halved and deseeded
- 3/4 lb ground lamb (340g)
- 1 1/2 cups fresh spinach, chopped (45g)
- 1/3 cup pitted olives, chopped (50g)
- 1/3 cup crumbled feta cheese (40g)
- 1/2 tsp dried oregano (0.6g)
- 2 tbsp olive oil (30ml)
- Salt and pepper to taste
- To Serve:
- 3/4 cup tzatziki sauce (180g)
- 2/3 cucumber, sliced (130g))

Instructions:

1. Preheat oven to 375°F (190°C). In a skillet, heat olive oil over medium heat. Add ground lamb and cook until browned, about 5-7 minutes. Season with salt, pepper, and oregano.
2. Stir in spinach and olives, cooking until spinach wilts. Remove from heat and mix in the crumbled feta.
3. Fill each bell pepper half with the lamb mixture. Place on a baking sheet and bake for 20 minutes, or until peppers are tender.
4. Serve with a side of tzatziki and cucumber slices.

Nutritional Facts (Per Serving): Calories: 600 | Sugars: 2g | Fat: 52g | Carbohydrates: 9g | Protein: 40g | Fiber: 5g | Sodium: 550mg

CHAPTER 9: LUNCHES: Keto Pasta and Risotto

Pesto Shirataki Spagetti

Prep: 5 minutes | Cook: 10 minutes | Serves: 2

Ingredients:

- 2 packages shirataki noodles, drained and rinsed (400g)
- 1/3 cup sugar-free, low-carb basil pesto (80g)
- 1/3 cup grated Parmesan cheese (40g)
- 2 tbsp olive oil (30ml)
- Salt and pepper to taste

Instructions:

1. In a skillet, heat olive oil over medium heat. Add the drained shirataki noodles and cook, stirring occasionally, for 3-4 minutes to remove any excess moisture and allow them to absorb the oil slightly.
2. Stir in the basil pesto, mixing well to coat the noodles evenly. Continue cooking for another 2-3 minutes, allowing the flavors to meld.
3. Season with salt and pepper as desired. Serve immediately, topped with grated Parmesan.

Nutritional Facts (Per Serving): Calories: 600 | Sugars: 1g | Fat: 52g | Carbohydrates: 8g | Protein: 26g | Fiber: 7g | Sodium: 450mg

Meatball and Cheese Keto Rigatoni

Prep: 15 minutes | Cook: 30 minutes | Serves: 2

Ingredients:

- 3/4 lb ground beef (340g)
- 1/2 cup shredded mozzarella cheese (60g)
- 1/3 cup grated Parmesan cheese (40g)
- 3/4 cup low-carb marinara sauce (180ml)
- 3/4 tsp Italian seasoning (1.5g)
- Salt and pepper to taste

Instructions:

1. In a bowl, season the ground beef with salt, pepper, and Italian seasoning. Form the mixture into small meatballs.
2. In a skillet over medium heat, add the meatballs and cook until browned on all sides, about 8 minutes, turning occasionally.
3. Pour the marinara sauce over the meatballs and bring to a simmer. Cover and cook for 10 minutes, allowing the meatballs to absorb the sauce flavors.
4. Stir in shredded mozzarella, allowing it to melt into the sauce. Serve hot, garnished with grated Parmesan.

Nutritional Facts (Per Serving): Calories: 600 | Sugars: 2g | Fat: 50g | Carbohydrates: 9g | Protein: 40g | Fiber: 5g | Sodium: 550mg

Chicken and Spinach Creamy Risotto

Prep: 10 minutes | Cook: 20 minutes | Serves: 2

Ingredients:

- 3/4 lb diced chicken breast (340g)
- 1 1/2 cups cauliflower rice (150g)
- 3/4 cup fresh spinach, chopped (45g)
- 1/3 cup heavy cream (80ml)
- 1/3 cup grated Parmesan cheese (40g)
- 2 tbsp olive oil (30ml)
- Salt and pepper to taste

Instructions:

1. Heat olive oil in a skillet over medium heat. Add diced chicken, seasoning with salt and pepper, and cook until browned, about 8 minutes. Remove chicken from the skillet and set aside.
2. In the same skillet, add cauliflower rice and cook for 3 minutes, stirring occasionally, until it starts to soften. Add the chopped spinach and cook for 1-2 minutes, or until wilted.
3. Return the chicken to the skillet, then pour in the heavy cream and sprinkle with Parmesan cheese.
4. Stir continuously for 2-3 minutes, until the mixture is creamy and well-combined. Serve warm.

Nutritional Facts (Per Serving): Calories: 600 | Sugars: 1g | Fat: 50g | Carbohydrates: 8g | Protein: 45g | Fiber: 5g | Sodium: 500mg

Bacon and Broccoli Keto Risotto

Prep: 10 minutes | Cook: 15 minutes | Serves: 2

Ingredients:

- 6 slices bacon, diced (90g)
- 1 1/4 cups broccoli florets, chopped (125g)
- 1 1/2 cups cauliflower rice (150g)
- 1/3 cup heavy cream (80ml)
- 1/3 cup grated Parmesan cheese (40g)
- 1 tbsp butter (15g)
- Salt and pepper to taste

Instructions:

1. In a skillet over medium heat, cook diced bacon until it becomes crispy, about 5 minutes. Use a slotted spoon to remove bacon, leaving the rendered fat in the skillet.
2. Add broccoli florets to the skillet with bacon fat, sautéing for 3-4 minutes until it begins to soften. Add cauliflower rice and cook for an additional 3-4 minutes, stirring occasionally.
3. Pour in the heavy cream and sprinkle with Parmesan cheese. Stir well to combine and cook for 2-3 minutes until the mixture becomes creamy, and the cheese melts into the sauce.
4. Stir the bacon back into the skillet, season with salt and pepper, and serve hot.

Nutritional Facts (Per Serving): Calories: 600 | Sugars: 1g | Fat: 52g | Carbohydrates: 9g | Protein: 35g | Fiber: 5g | Sodium: 600mg

CHAPTER 10: LUNCHES: Gourmet Keto Meats

Mediterranean Chicken & Vegetable Skewers with Tzatziki Sauce

Prep: 15 minutes | Cook: 15 minutes | Serves: 2

Ingredients:

- 2/3 lb chicken breast, cubed (300g)
- 2/3 zucchini, sliced (90g)
- 2/3 red bell pepper, cubed (90g)
- 1/3 red onion, cubed (60g)
- 1 1/2 tbsp olive oil (22ml)
- 1 tsp dried oregano (0.7g)
- Salt and pepper to taste

Tzatziki Sauce:
- 3/4 cup full-fat, unsweetened Greek yogurt (180g)
- 1/2 cucumber, grated and drained (100g)
- 1 1/2 cloves garlic, minced
- 1 1/2 tbsp fresh dill, chopped (6g)
- Salt and pepper to taste

Instructions:

1. In a bowl, combine olive oil, oregano, salt, and pepper. Add cubed chicken and toss to coat. Thread chicken, zucchini, bell pepper, and red onion onto skewers.
2. Preheat grill or grill pan to medium-high heat. Grill skewers for 10-12 minutes.
3. For the tzatziki sauce, mix Greek yogurt, grated cucumber, minced garlic, and dill in a small bowl. Season with salt and pepper. Serve skewers with tzatziki on the side.

Nutritional Facts (Per Serving): Calories: 550 | Sugars: 2g | Fat: 42g | Carbohydrates: 7g | Protein: 45g | Fiber: 3g | Sodium: 480mg

Grilled Chicken Breast with Lemon Butter Sauce

Prep: 10 minutes | Cook: 20 minutes | Serves: 2

Ingredients:

- 2 medium chicken breasts (220g each)
- Salt and pepper to taste
- 1 1/2 tbsp olive oil (22ml)

Lemon Butter Sauce:
- 3 tbsp butter (45g)
- 1 1/2 tbsp lemon juice (22ml)
- 2 cloves garlic, minced
- 1 1/2 tsp fresh parsley, chopped (2g)

Instructions:

1. Season chicken breasts with salt and pepper. Heat olive oil in a grill pan over medium heat. Grill chicken breasts for 6-8 minutes per side, until fully cooked and juices run clear.
2. In a small saucepan, melt butter over low heat. Add garlic and cook until fragrant, about 1 minute. Stir in lemon juice and parsley, then remove from heat.
3. Drizzle lemon butter sauce over grilled chicken and serve immediately.

Nutritional Facts (Per Serving): Calories: 580 | Sugars: 1g | Fat: 48g | Carbohydrates: 4g | Protein: 50g | Fiber: 1g | Sodium: 420mg

Garlic Herb Lamb Chops with Cauliflower Mash and Fresh Thyme

Prep: 10 minutes | Cook: 25 minutes | Serves: 2

Ingredients:

- 4 small lamb chops (300g)
- 2 cloves garlic, minced
- 1 1/2 tbsp olive oil (22ml)
- 1 1/2 tsp fresh thyme leaves (0.8g)
- 1 1/2 cups cauliflower florets (200g)
- 3 tbsp butter (45g)
- Salt and pepper to taste

Instructions:

1. Combine minced garlic, olive oil, thyme, salt, and pepper, then rub the mixture evenly over the lamb chops. Let marinate for 10 minutes.
2. Heat a skillet over medium-high heat and cook the lamb chops for 3-4 minutes per side, or until they reach your desired doneness. Set aside to rest.
3. Steam cauliflower florets for about 10 minutes until tender, then drain and combine with butter, salt, and pepper. Mash until smooth.
4. Serve the lamb chops with cauliflower mash, garnished with extra thyme if desired.

Nutritional Facts (Per Serving): Calories: 580 | Sugars: 1g | Fat: 50g | Carbohydrates: 7g | Protein: 38g | Fiber: 4g | Sodium: 450mg

Keto Pork and Pistachio Meat Fingers

Prep: 15 minutes | Cook: 20 minutes | Serves: 2

Ingredients:

- 3/4 lb ground pork (340g)
- 1/3 cup pistachios, finely chopped (40g)
- 1 large egg, beaten
- 1 1/4 tsp garlic powder (4g)
- Salt and pepper to taste
- 1 1/2 tbsp olive oil (22ml)
- Optional Dipping Sauce:
- 3 tbsp Greek yogurt (45g)
- 1 1/2 tsp Dijon mustard (7g)

Instructions:

1. In a bowl, mix ground pork, chopped pistachios, beaten egg, garlic powder, salt, and pepper until evenly combined. Shape the mixture into finger-sized pieces.
2. Heat olive oil in a skillet over medium heat. Cook the meat fingers for 8-10 minutes, turning occasionally, until browned on all sides and cooked through.
3. For the dipping sauce, mix greek yogurt and Dijon mustard in a small bowl. Serve meat fingers with the sauce and a side of vegetables or a salad.

Nutritional Facts (Per Serving): Calories: 590 | Sugars: 1g | Fat: 50g | Carbohydrates: 8g | Protein: 40g | Fiber: 3g | Sodium: 500mg

Tuscan Chicken Thighs with Spinach and Sun-Dried Tomatoes

Prep: 10 minutes | Cook: 25 minutes | Serves: 2

Ingredients:

- 5 boneless, skinless chicken thighs (500g)
- 2 1/2 cups fresh spinach (75g)
- 1/3 cup sun-dried tomatoes in olive oil, chopped (50g)
- 2/3 cup heavy cream (160ml)
- 1 1/2 tbsp olive oil (22ml)
- Salt and pepper to taste

Instructions:

1. Heat olive oil in a skillet over medium heat. Season the chicken thighs with salt and pepper, then cook for 5-7 minutes per side until golden and cooked through. Remove chicken and set aside.
2. In the same skillet, add sun-dried tomatoes and cook for about 1 minute until they start to soften. Add spinach and cook for another 1-2 minutes, stirring until wilted.
3. Pour in the heavy cream, stirring continuously until the sauce slightly thickens, about 2-3 minutes. Return the chicken thighs to the skillet, spooning the sauce over them. Let simmer for 2-3 more minutes, then serve warm.

Nutritional Facts (Per Serving): Calories: 590 | Sugars: 1g | Fat: 48g | Carbohydrates: 8g | Protein: 45g | Fiber: 3g | Sodium: 500mg

Beef Tenderloin with Creamed Spinach

Prep: 10 minutes | Cook: 20 minutes | Serves: 2

Ingredients:

- 2 beef tenderloin steaks (225g each)
- 1 1/2 tbsp olive oil (22ml)
- 3 cups fresh spinach (90g)
- 1/3 cup heavy cream (80ml)
- 1/3 cup grated Parmesan cheese (40g)
- Salt and pepper to taste

Instructions:

1. Season tenderloin steaks with salt and pepper. Heat olive oil in a skillet over medium-high heat and cook steaks for 4-5 minutes per side for medium-rare, or adjust to your preferred doneness. Remove steaks from skillet and let rest.
2. In the same skillet, add spinach and cook, stirring frequently, until wilted, about 2 minutes. Pour in heavy cream and sprinkle with Parmesan cheese, stirring until the mixture thickens and becomes creamy, about 3-4 minutes.
3. Serve the steaks topped with the creamed spinach, and garnish with extra Parmesan if desired.

Nutritional Facts (Per Serving): Calories: 600 | Sugars: 1g | Fat: 52g | Carbohydrates: 6g | Protein: 48g | Fiber: 2g | Sodium: 480mg

Herbed Lamb Kofta with Mint Yogurt Sauce

Prep: 15 minutes | Cook: 25 minutes | Serves: 2

Ingredients:

- 9 oz ground lamb (260g)
- 1 1/2 tbsp olive oil (22ml)
- 2 cloves garlic, minced (10g)
- 3 tbsp fresh mint, chopped (15g)
- 3/4 tsp cumin (3g)
- 3/4 tsp coriander (3g)
- Salt and pepper to taste
- For the Sauce:
- 1/2 cup Greek yogurt (120g)
- 1 1/2 tsp lemon juice (7ml)
- 1 1/2 tbsp fresh mint, chopped (7g)

Instructions:

1. In a bowl, combine ground lamb, garlic, fresh mint, cumin, coriander, salt, and pepper. Mix well and form into small oval-shaped koftas.
2. Heat olive oil in a skillet over medium heat. Cook the koftas for about 10 minutes, turning occasionally until browned and cooked through.
3. In a small bowl, mix Greek yogurt, lemon juice, and mint for the sauce.
4. Serve the koftas with mint yogurt sauce and enjoy!

Nutritional Facts (Per Serving): Calories: 580 | Carbohydrates: 6g | Protein: 45g | Fat: 48g | Fiber: 1g | Sodium: 500mg | Sugars: 3g

Keto BBQ Chicken Thighs with Apple Cabbage Slaw

Prep: 10 minutes | Cook: 30 minutes | Serves: 2

Ingredients:

- 3 bone-in, skin-on chicken thighs (340g)
- 3 tbsp sugar-free BBQ sauce (45ml)
- 3/4 cup shredded cabbage (75g)
- 1/3 green apple, thinly sliced (50g)
- 2 tbsp Greek yogurt (30g)
- 3/4 tsp apple cider vinegar (3.5ml)
- Salt and pepper to taste

Instructions:

1. Preheat oven to 400°F (200°C). Season chicken thighs with salt and pepper, then brush each thigh with BBQ sauce, coating evenly. Place on a baking sheet and bake for 30 minutes, or until the chicken is cooked through, and the BBQ sauce is caramelized.
2. While the chicken is baking, prepare the slaw by combining shredded cabbage, sliced apple, greek yogurt, and apple cider vinegar in a mixing bowl. Season with salt and pepper, then toss well to combine.
3. Serve the BBQ chicken thighs with a side of apple cabbage slaw.

Nutritional Facts (Per Serving): Calories: 590 | Carbohydrates: 9g | Protein: 58g | Fat: 40g | Fiber: 3g | Sodium: 650mg | Sugars: 5g

Ultimate Grilled Beef Burger with Aged Cheddar, Avocado & Caramelized Onions

Prep: 15 minutes | Cook: 15 minutes | Serves: 2

Ingredients:

- 3/4 lb ground beef (340g)
- Salt and pepper to taste
- 2 slices aged cheddar (40g)
- 3/4 avocado, sliced (110g)
- 2/3 onion, thinly sliced (80g)
- 1 1/2 tbsp butter (22g)
- 4 large lettuce leaves (for wrapping)

Instructions:

1. Form the ground beef into two equal-sized patties, seasoning both sides with salt and pepper. Preheat a grill or grill pan over medium-high heat and cook the patties for about 4-5 minutes per side. Add a slice of cheddar to each patty during the last minute of cooking to melt the cheese.
2. Melt butter in a skillet over medium heat. Add sliced onions and cook, stirring occasionally, until they become golden brown, about 8 minutes.
3. To assemble, place each cooked patty on a large lettuce leaf. Top with avocado slices and caramelized onions, then wrap with the lettuce to secure.

Nutritional Facts (Per Serving): Calories: 580 | Sugars: 2g | Fat: 50g | Carbohydrates: 7g | Protein: 42g | Fiber: 4g | Sodium: 450mg

Garlic Herb Butter-Crispy Chicken Drumsticks with Lemon Zest

Prep: 10 minutes | Cook: 40 minutes | Serves: 2

Ingredients:

- 5 chicken drumsticks (550g)
- 2 1/2 tbsp butter, melted (37g)
- 3 cloves garlic, minced
- 1 1/2 tsp lemon zest (3g)
- 1 1/2 tsp fresh rosemary, chopped (1.5g)
- Salt and pepper to taste

Instructions:

1. Preheat the oven to 400°F (200°C). In a small bowl, combine melted butter, minced garlic, lemon zest, chopped rosemary, salt, and pepper, mixing well.
2. Place the drumsticks on a baking sheet and brush them generously with the garlic herb butter, coating each drumstick evenly. Reserve a small amount of butter for basting.
3. Roast the drumsticks in the oven for 35-40 minutes, basting with the remaining butter halfway through, until the skin is crispy, and the meat is cooked through. Serve warm, garnished with additional lemon zest if desired.

Nutritional Facts (Per Serving): Calories: 600 | Sugars: 1g | Fat: 52g | Carbohydrates: 4g | Protein: 48g | Fiber: 1g | Sodium: 400mg

Herb-Crusted Pork Chops with Lemon Zest

Prep: 15 minutes | Cook: 45 minutes | Serves: 2

Ingredients:

- 2 bone-in pork chops (500g total)
- 1 1/2 tbsp olive oil (22ml)
- 1/3 cup grated Parmesan cheese (40g)
- 1 tsp lemon zest (2g)
- 1 tsp dried oregano (1g)
- 1 tsp dried thyme (1g)
- Salt and pepper to taste

Instructions:

1. Preheat oven to 375°F (190°C). Line a baking sheet with parchment paper.
2. In a small bowl, mix Parmesan, lemon zest, oregano, thyme, salt, and pepper.
3. Brush olive oil evenly over the pork chops, then press the herb mixture onto both sides.
4. Heat a skillet over medium-high heat and sear the pork chops for 2 minutes per side until golden brown.
5. Transfer the pork chops to the baking sheet and roast in the oven for 15-20 minutes, or until the internal temperature reaches 145°F (63°C).
6. Let the pork chops rest for 5 minutes, then serve warm.

Nutritional Facts (Per Serving): Calories: 580 | Sugars: 1g | Fat: 45g | Carbohydrates: 5g | Protein: 50g | Fiber: 1g | Sodium: 500mg

Grana Padano-Crusted Chicken with Zucchini

Prep: 10 minutes | Cook: 20 minutes | Serves: 2

Ingredients:

- 2 large chicken breasts, pounded thin (225g each)
- 1/3 cup grated Grana Padano cheese (40g)
- 1 large zucchini, sliced (200g)
- 1 1/2 tbsp olive oil (22ml)
- Salt and pepper to taste

Instructions:

1. Preheat the oven to 400°F (200°C). Season both sides of the chicken breasts with salt and pepper, then press grated Grana Padano cheese onto one side of each chicken breast, pressing gently to adhere.
2. Heat olive oil in an oven-safe skillet over medium heat. Place the chicken in the skillet, cheese-side down, and cook for 3-4 minutes until the cheese forms a golden crust. Flip the chicken, add zucchini slices around it, and transfer the skillet to the oven.
3. Bake for 10-12 minutes, or until the chicken is cooked through and zucchini is tender. Serve warm, garnished with extra cheese if desired.

Nutritional Facts (Per Serving): Calories: 580 | Sugars: 1g | Fat: 42g | Carbohydrates: 6g | Protein: 50g | Fiber: 2g | Sodium: 500mg

CHAPTER 11: SNACKS: Keto Light Treats

Zesty Lemon Herb Chicken Wings

Prep: 10 minutes | **Cook:** 25 minutes | **Serves:** 4

Ingredients:

- 1 lb chicken wings (450g)
- 2 tbsp olive oil (30ml)
- 1 tbsp lemon juice (15ml)
- 1 tsp lemon zest (5g)
- 1 tsp fresh rosemary, chopped (5g)
- 1 tsp fresh thyme, chopped (5g)
- 1/2 tsp garlic powder (2.5g)
- Salt and pepper to taste

Instructions:

1. Preheat oven to 400°F (200°C).
2. In a large bowl, mix olive oil, lemon juice, lemon zest, rosemary, thyme, garlic powder, salt, and pepper.
3. Toss chicken wings in the mixture until well-coated.
4. Arrange wings on a baking sheet lined with parchment paper.
5. Bake for 20-25 minutes, turning halfway through, until golden and crispy.

Nutritional Facts (Per Serving): Calories: 250 | Carbohydrates: 3g | Protein: 15g | Fat: 20g | Fiber: 3g | Sodium: 175mg | Sugars: 0g

Jalapeño Poppers with Cream Cheese and Crispy Prosciutto

Prep: 15 minutes | **Cook:** 20 minutes | **Serves:** 4

Ingredients:

- 8 large jalapeño peppers (100g)
- 4 oz cream cheese, softened (115g)
- 4 slices prosciutto, halved (40g)
- 1/4 tsp garlic powder (1g)
- 1/4 tsp onion powder (1g)

Instructions:

1. Preheat oven to 375°F (190°C).
2. Slice jalapeños in half lengthwise and remove seeds.
3. In a bowl, mix cream cheese with garlic and onion powders.
4. Fill each jalapeño half with cream cheese mixture and wrap with a slice of prosciutto.
5. Place on a baking sheet and bake for 15-20 minutes until prosciutto is crispy.

Nutritional Facts (Per Serving): Calories: 250 | Carbohydrates: 2g | Protein: 13g | Fat: 21g | Fiber: 3g | Sodium: 180mg | Sugars: 1g

Eggplant Involtini with Ricotta and Basil

Prep: 20 minutes | Cook: 30 minutes | Serves: 4

Ingredients:

- 1 medium eggplant, thinly sliced (250g)
- 1 cup ricotta cheese (240g)
- 1/4 cup fresh basil, chopped (10g)
- 1/4 cup grated Parmesan (20g)
- 1/4 tsp garlic powder (1g)
- Salt and pepper to taste
- 2 tbsp olive oil (30ml)

Instructions:

1. Preheat the oven to 375°F (190°C). Brush both sides of the eggplant slices with olive oil and lightly season with salt. Heat a grill pan over medium-high heat and grill each slice until softened and slightly charred, about 2 minutes per side. Set the eggplant aside to cool slightly.
2. In a mixing bowl, combine the ricotta, basil, Parmesan, garlic powder, salt, and pepper. Stir until the mixture is smooth and well-blended. Place a spoonful of the ricotta mixture on one end of each eggplant slice, then carefully roll up the slice.
3. Arrange the eggplant rolls in a baking dish, seam side down, and bake for 15-20 minutes until heated through and lightly golden on top. Serve warm.

Nutritional Facts (Per Serving): Calories: 250 | Carbohydrates: 3g | Protein: 15g | Fat: 20g | Fiber: 3g | Sodium: 190mg | Sugars: 1g

Crispy Halloumi Fries with Herb Dipping Sauce

Prep: 10 minutes | Cook: 10 minutes | Serves: 4

Ingredients:

- 8 oz halloumi cheese, cut into fries (225g)
- 2 tbsp olive oil (30ml)
- 1/4 cup Greek yogurt (60g)
- 1 tbsp fresh parsley, chopped (5g)
- 1 tsp lemon juice (5ml)
- 1/2 tsp dried oregano (2g)
- Salt and pepper to taste

Instructions:

1. Heat olive oil in a non-stick skillet over medium heat. Once hot, add the halloumi fries in a single layer, ensuring they don't touch. Cook, turning occasionally, until all sides are golden and crispy, about 2-3 minutes per side. Remove from the skillet and drain on paper towels if needed.
2. While the halloumi fries are cooking, prepare the dipping sauce. In a small bowl, combine the Greek yogurt, parsley, lemon juice, oregano, salt, and pepper, mixing until smooth and well-blended. Serve the hot halloumi fries with the herb dipping sauce on the side.

Nutritional Facts (Per Serving): Calories: 250 | Carbohydrates: 2g | Protein: 15g | Fat: 20g | Fiber: 3g | Sodium: 180mg | Sugars: 0g

Cheesy Cauliflower Tots with Spicy Ranch Dip

Prep: 10 minutes | Cook: 25 minutes | Serves: 2

Ingredients:

- 1 cup cauliflower florets, steamed and mashed (150g)
- 1/4 cup shredded cheddar cheese (30g)
- 1 tbsp almond flour (7g)
- 1 large egg white (25g)
- 1/4 tsp garlic powder (1g)
- Salt and pepper to taste
- 1/2 tbsp olive oil (7g)
- For the Dip:
- 2 tbsp Greek yogurt, full-fat (30g)
- 1/2 tsp hot sauce (2g)
- 1/4 tsp smoked paprika (1g)

Instructions:

1. Preheat oven to 400°F (200°C). Line a baking sheet with parchment paper.
2. In a bowl, mix mashed cauliflower, cheese, almond flour, egg white, garlic powder, salt, and pepper. Shape into small tots.
3. Brush with olive oil and bake for 15-20 minutes, flipping halfway, until golden and crisp.
4. Meanwhile, mix yogurt, hot sauce, and paprika for the dip.
5. Serve the cauliflower tots with spicy ranch dip.

Nutritional Facts (Per Serving): Calories: 250 | Fat: 17g | Carbs: 6g | Fiber: 3g | Protein: 14g | Sugars: 2g | Sodium: 320mg

Creamy Spinach and Artichoke Dip Bites

Prep: 15 minutes | Cook: 20 minutes | Serves: 4

Ingredients:

- 1/2 cup cream cheese, softened (120g)
- 1/2 cup cooked spinach, chopped and squeezed dry (60g)
- 1/4 cup marinated artichoke hearts, chopped (50g)
- 1/3 cup grated Parmesan (30g)
- 1/2 tsp garlic powder (2g)
- Salt and pepper to taste
- 8 mini bell peppers, halved and deseeded (150g)

Instructions:

1. Preheat the oven to 375°F (190°C) and line a baking sheet with parchment paper. Arrange the mini bell pepper halves on the baking sheet, cut side up.
2. In a mixing bowl, combine the cream cheese, spinach, artichoke hearts, Parmesan, garlic powder, salt, and pepper.
3. Spoon the filling evenly into each bell pepper half, filling them just to the top.
4. Bake for 15-20 minutes, or until the filling is heated through, and the tops are lightly golden. Let cool briefly before serving.

Nutritional Facts (Per Serving): Calories: 250 | Carbohydrates: 2g | Protein: 13g | Fat: 21g | Fiber: 2g | Sodium: 170mg | Sugars: 1g

CHAPTER 12: SNACKS: Keto Sauces & Spreads

Creamy Avocado Cilantro Lime Dip

Prep: 10 minutes | Cook: 2 minutes | Serves: 4

Ingredients:

- 1 large avocado, peeled and pitted (200g)
- 1/4 cup sour cream (60g)
- 1/4 cup fresh cilantro, chopped (10g)
- 1 tbsp lime juice (15ml)
- 1/2 tsp garlic powder (2g)
- Salt and pepper to taste

Instructions:

1. Place the avocado, sour cream, cilantro, lime juice, and garlic powder in a blender or food processor.
2. Blend on high until the mixture is completely smooth and creamy, scraping down the sides as needed.
3. Season with salt and pepper, adjusting to taste, and blend briefly to combine.
4. Transfer the dip to a serving bowl and garnish with extra cilantro, if desired. Serve chilled with low-carb chips or fresh vegetable sticks for dipping.

Nutritional Facts (Per Serving): Calories: 250 | Carbohydrates: 3g | Protein: 3g | Fat: 23g | Fiber: 4g | Sodium: 150mg | Sugars: 0g

Keto Pesto Parmesan Dip

Prep: 5 minutes | Cook: 2 minutes | Serves: 4

Ingredients:

- 1/2 cup greek yogurt (120g)
- 1/4 cup grated Parmesan cheese (20g)
- 2 tbsp basil pesto (30g)
- 1 tbsp lemon juice (15ml)
- Salt and pepper to taste

Instructions:

1. In a mixing bowl, combine the greek yogurt, Parmesan cheese, basil pesto, and lemon juice.
2. Stir the mixture thoroughly until smooth and all ingredients are evenly blended.
3. Taste and adjust seasoning with salt and pepper as desired for a balanced flavor.
4. Transfer the dip to a serving dish and garnish with a sprinkle of Parmesan or fresh basil for a decorative touch. Serve with low-carb crackers or fresh vegetable sticks.

Nutritional Facts (Per Serving): Calories: 250 | Carbohydrates: 2g | Protein: 4g | Fat: 24g | Fiber: 0g | Sodium: 180mg | Sugars: 0g

Spicy Avocado Jalapeño Cream Sauce

Prep: 5 minutes | Cook: 2 minutes | Serves: 4

Ingredients:

- 1/2 ripe avocado (75g)
- 1/4 cup sour cream (60g)
- 1 tbsp fresh lime juice (15ml)
- 1 small jalapeño, deseeded and chopped (15g)
- 1 tbsp fresh cilantro, chopped (5g)
- 1/2 tsp garlic powder (1g)
- Salt and pepper to taste

Instructions:

1. In a blender, combine avocado, sour cream, lime juice, jalapeño, cilantro, garlic powder, salt, and pepper.
2. Blend until smooth and creamy. Adjust seasoning if needed.
3. Serve as a dip for grilled meats, tacos, or roasted veggies.

Nutritional Facts (Per Serving): Calories: 250 | Fat: 22g | Carbs: 4g | Fiber: 2g | Protein: 2g | Sodium: 150mg

Garlic Parmesan Herb Dip

Prep: 10 minutes | Cook: 2 minutes | Serves: 4

Ingredients:

- 1/2 cup Greek yogurt, full-fat (120g)
- 1/4 cup sour cream (60g)
- 2 tbsp grated Parmesan cheese (15g)
- 1 tbsp fresh chives, chopped (5g)
- 1/2 tsp garlic powder (1g)
- 1/4 tsp smoked paprika (1g)
- Salt and pepper to taste

Instructions:

1. In a bowl, mix Greek yogurt, sour cream, Parmesan, chives, garlic powder, paprika, salt, and pepper.
2. Stir until smooth and well combined. Let rest for 5 minutes to enhance flavors.
3. Serve with fresh veggies, keto crackers, or grilled meats.

Nutritional Facts (Per Serving): Calories: 250 | Fat: 22g | Carbs: 3g | Fiber: 0g | Protein: 5g | Sodium: 180mg

Roasted Red Pepper and Feta Spread

Prep: 5 minutes | Cook: 2 minutes | Serves: 4

Ingredients:

- 1/2 cup roasted red peppers, drained (120g)
- 1/2 cup feta cheese, crumbled (60g)
- 2 tbsp olive oil (30ml)
- 1 clove garlic, minced (3g)
- 1 tsp lemon juice (5ml)
- Salt and pepper to taste

Instructions:

1. Blend all ingredients in a food processor until smooth and creamy.
2. Taste and adjust seasoning if needed.
3. Serve as a dip for veggies, keto crackers, or grilled meats.

Nutritional Facts (Per Serving): Calories: 250 | Fat: 22g | Carbs: 3g | Protein: 5g | Fiber: 1g | Sodium: 300mg

Cilantro Lime Yogurt Sauce

Prep: 10 minutes | Cook: 2 minutes | Serves: 4

Ingredients:

- 1/2 cup Greek yogurt, full-fat (120g)
- 1/4 cup sour cream (60g)
- 1 tbsp lime juice (15ml)
- 2 tbsp fresh cilantro, chopped (10g)
- 1/2 tsp garlic powder (1g)
- 1/4 tsp cumin (1g)
- Salt and pepper to taste

Instructions:

1. In a small bowl, whisk all ingredients until well combined.
2. Adjust seasoning as needed.
3. Serve with grilled meats, seafood, or as a dip for keto-friendly snacks.

Nutritional Facts (Per Serving): Calories: 250 | Fat: 22g | Carbs: 2g | Protein: 4g | Fiber: 0g | Sodium: 150mg

CHAPTER 13: DESSERTS: Low-Carb Indulgences

Raspberry & Coconut Cream Parfaits with Chia Seeds

Prep: 15 minutes | Chill: 1 hour | Serves: 4

Ingredients:

- 1 cup coconut cream (240g)
- 1/2 cup fresh raspberries (60g)
- 1 tbsp chia seeds (15g)
- 1/4 tsp vanilla extract (1ml)
- Low carb sweetener to taste

Instructions:

1. In a mixing bowl, combine the coconut cream, vanilla extract, and low-carb sweetener, whisking until smooth. Stir in the chia seeds and let sit for 5 minutes to thicken slightly.
2. Spoon a layer of the coconut cream mixture and raspberries into the bottom of each serving glass. Repeat layers until all ingredients are used.
3. Cover and refrigerate for at least 1 hour.
4. Garnish with extra raspberries and a sprinkle of chia seeds before serving. Serve chilled.

Nutritional Facts (Per Serving): Calories: 250 | Carbohydrates: 3g | Protein: 3g | Fat: 23g | Fiber: 4g | Sodium: 125mg | Sugars: 0g

Chocolate Almond Protein Bars

Prep: 10 minutes | Chill: 1 hour | Serves: 4

Ingredients:

- 1/2 cup almond flour (60g)
- 2 tbsp cocoa powder (15g)
- 1/4 cup chocolate protein powder (30g)
- 1/4 cup almond butter (60g)
- 2 tbsp low-carb sweetener (20g)
- 2 tbsp unsweetened almond milk (30ml)

Instructions:

1. In a large bowl, combine the almond flour, cocoa powder, and chocolate protein powder.
2. Add the almond butter, low-carb sweetener, and almond milk, stirring until a thick dough forms. The mixture should be firm enough to hold its shape when pressed.
3. Press the dough evenly into a lined baking dish, smoothing the top with the back of a spoon.
4. Refrigerate for at least 1 hour until firm. Cut into bars and serve.

Nutritional Facts (Per Serving): Calories: 250 | Carbohydrates: 3g | Protein: 15g | Fat: 20g | Fiber: 3g | Sodium: 125mg | Sugars: 0g

Sugar-Free Walnut & Dark Chocolate Cream Cheese Truffles

Prep: 15 minutes | Chill: 1 hour | Serves: 4

Ingredients:

- 1/2 cup cream cheese, softened (120g)
- 1/4 cup finely chopped walnuts (30g)
- 1/4 cup dark chocolate, chopped (30g)
- 1/2 tsp vanilla extract (2ml)
- Low carb sweetener to taste

Instructions:

1. In a mixing bowl, beat the softened cream cheese until it becomes light and smooth. Add the vanilla extract and low-carb sweetener. Mix well.
2. Fold in the chopped walnuts and dark chocolate, distributing them evenly throughout the cream cheese mixture. The nuts and chocolate should be in small pieces.
3. Using a spoon, portion out the mixture and roll it into small, bite-sized balls with your hands. Place each truffle on a tray lined with parchment paper. For a firmer texture, place the tray in the freezer for about 10-15 minutes before handling.
4. After shaping, refrigerate the truffles for at least 1 hour. Serve chilled, and garnish with a sprinkle of chopped walnuts or a dusting of cocoa powder.

Nutritional Facts (Per Serving): Calories: 250 | Carbohydrates: 3g | Protein: 5g | Fat: 22g | Fiber: 3g | Sodium: 125mg | Sugars: 0g

Spiced Berry Crumble "Bonfai Toffee" with Almond Flour Crust

Prep: 15 minutes | Cook: 25 minutes | Serves: 4

Ingredients:

For the Filling:
- 1 cup fresh blackberries or raspberries (100g)
- 1/4 tsp cinnamon (1g)
- 1/4 tsp nutmeg (1g)
- 2 tbsp low-carb sweetener (20g)
- 1 tbsp butter (15g)

For the Crust:
- 1 cup almond flour (120g)
- 2 tbsp melted butter (30g)
- 1 tbsp low-carb sweetener (10g)

Instructions:

1. Preheat the oven to 350°F (175°C). In a small bowl, mix almond flour, melted butter, and low-carb sweetener for the crust. Press this mixture evenly into the bottom of a small baking dish.
2. In a saucepan, melt the butter over medium heat. Add the blackberries (or raspberries), cinnamon, nutmeg, and sweetener. Stir and cook for 3-5 minutes until the berries are softened.
3. Pour the spiced berry mixture over the almond crust, spreading it evenly.
4. Bake in the preheated oven for 20-25 minutes. Let cool slightly before serving.

Nutritional Facts (Per Serving): Calories: 250 | Carbohydrates: 3g | Protein: 6g | Fat: 22g | Fiber: 5g | Sodium: 130mg | Sugars: 1g

Keto Vanilla Bean Panna Cotta

Prep: 10 minutes | Chill: 2 hours | Serves: 4

Ingredients:

- 1 cup heavy cream (240ml)
- 1/2 cup unsweetened almond milk (120ml)
- 1 tsp vanilla bean paste or 1 vanilla bean, seeds scraped (5ml)
- 1 tbsp powdered low-carb sweetener (10g)
- 1/2 tsp gelatin powder (2.5g)

Instructions:

1. In a small saucepan, heat the heavy cream, almond milk, vanilla bean paste (or scraped seeds), and low-carb sweetener over medium heat, stirring occasionally until just starting to simmer. Do not let it boil.
2. Sprinkle the gelatin powder over 1 tbsp of water in a small bowl to bloom for a minute, then stir into the hot cream mixture until fully dissolved.
3. Remove from heat and let the mixture cool slightly. Pour the panna cotta mixture evenly into small serving glasses or ramekins.
4. Chill in the refrigerator for at least 2 hours, or until set. Serve cold, garnished with fresh berries or a sprinkle of unsweetened shredded coconut.

Nutritional Facts (Per Serving): Calories: 250 | Carbohydrates: 3g | Protein: 4g | Fat: 23g | Fiber: 0g | Sodium: 125mg | Sugars: 0g

Mocha Hazelnut Keto Bites

Prep: 15 minutes | Chill: 1 hour | Serves: 4

Ingredients:

- 1/2 cup hazelnut flour (60g)
- 1 tbsp cocoa powder (7g)
- 1/4 cup coconut oil, melted (60ml)
- 1 tbsp espresso powder (5g)
- 2 tbsp low-carb sweetener (20g)
- 1/4 tsp vanilla extract (1ml)

Instructions:

1. In a mixing bowl, combine the hazelnut flour, cocoa powder, espresso powder, and low-carb sweetener. Stir until the dry ingredients are well-blended.
2. Add the melted coconut oil and vanilla extract, stirring until the mixture forms a smooth, moldable dough.
3. Roll the dough into small balls, using your hands to shape them evenly. Place each bite on a tray lined with parchment paper.
4. Refrigerate for at least 1 hour to firm up. Serve chilled and garnish with a dusting of cocoa powder or a few chopped hazelnuts if desired.

Nutritional Facts (Per Serving): Calories: 250 | Carbohydrates: 3g | Protein: 5g | Fat: 23g | Fiber: 3g | Sodium: 130mg | Sugars: 0g

Keto Tiramisu with Mascarpone Cream

Prep: 20 minutes | Chill: 2 hours | Serves: 4

Ingredients:

- 1/2 cup mascarpone cheese (120g)
- 1/2 cup heavy cream (120ml)
- 1 tbsp brewed espresso, cooled (15ml)
- 1/4 tsp cocoa powder, for dusting (1g)
- 1 tbsp powdered low-carb sweetener (10g)
- 1/2 tsp vanilla extract (2.5ml)

Instructions:

1. In a mixing bowl, whip the heavy cream with the powdered sweetener and vanilla extract until soft peaks form.
2. In a separate bowl, beat the mascarpone until smooth. Fold the whipped cream gently into the mascarpone until fully combined.
3. Layer the mascarpone mixture into small serving glasses, adding a light drizzle of espresso between layers to give a classic tiramisu flavor.
4. Dust the top of each serving with a sprinkle of cocoa powder. Chill for at least 2 hours to set before serving.

Nutritional Facts (Per Serving): Calories: 250 | Carbohydrates: 3g | Protein: 4g | Fat: 23g | Fiber: 0g | Sodium: 125mg | Sugars: 0g

Pumpkin Spice Cheesecake Bites

Prep: 15 minutes | Chill: 1 hour | Serves: 4

Ingredients:

- 1/2 cup cream cheese, softened (120g)
- 1/4 cup pumpkin purée (60g)
- 1/4 tsp pumpkin spice (1g)
- 1 tbsp powdered low-carb sweetener (10g)
- 1/4 tsp vanilla extract (1ml)

Instructions:

1. In a medium mixing bowl, add the softened cream cheese and pumpkin purée. Beat with a hand mixer or whisk until the mixture is smooth and free of any lumps.
2. Add the pumpkin spice, powdered low-carb sweetener, and vanilla extract to the bowl. Mix thoroughly until all ingredients are evenly distributed.
3. Using a spoon or small cookie scoop, portion out the mixture into small bite-sized balls. Roll each portion between your palms to create smooth, even spheres, and place them on a parchment-lined tray.
4. Refrigerate the tray of cheesecake bites for at least 1 hour, or until they are firm to the touch. Before serving, sprinkle a light dusting of pumpkin spice or cinnamon over each bite. Serve chilled.

Nutritional Facts (Per Serving): Calories: 250 | Carbohydrates: 3g | Protein: 4g | Fat: 22g | Fiber: 3g | Sodium: 130mg | Sugars: 0g

CHAPTER 14: DESSERTS: Festive Keto Desserts

Sugar-Free Lemon Tart

Prep: 15 minutes | Cook: 25 minutes | Serves: 4

Ingredients:

For the Filling:
- 1/2 cup lemon juice (120ml)
- 2 tbsp lemon zest (10g)
- 3 large eggs
- 1/4 cup powdered low-carb sweetener (30g)
- 1/4 cup heavy cream (60ml)

For the Crust:
- 1 cup almond flour (120g)
- 2 tbsp melted butter (30g)
- 1 tbsp powdered low-carb sweetener (10g)

Instructions:

1. Preheat oven to 350°F (175°C). In a small bowl, combine almond flour, melted butter, and sweetener for the crust. Press the mixture into a tart pan, creating an even layer.
2. Bake the crust for 8-10 minutes. Let it cool.
3. Whisk together the lemon juice, zest, eggs, sweetener, and heavy cream. Pour it into the crust.
4. Bake for 15-20 minutes until the filling is set but still slightly jiggly in the center. Cool completely, then refrigerate for at least 1 hour before serving.

Nutritional Facts (Per Serving): Calories: 250 | Carbohydrates: 3g | Protein: 5g | Fat: 22g | Fiber: 3g | Sodium: 125mg | Sugars: 0g

Coconut Flour Brownies

Prep: 10 minutes | Cook: 25 minutes | Serves: 4

Ingredients:

- 1/4 cup coconut flour (30g)
- 1/4 cup cocoa powder (25g)
- 1/2 cup melted butter (120g)
- 3 large eggs
- 1/4 cup powdered low-carb sweetener (30g)
- 1/2 tsp vanilla extract (2.5ml)

Instructions:

1. Preheat oven to 350°F (175°C) and line a small baking dish with parchment paper.
2. In a mixing bowl, whisk together the melted butter, eggs, sweetener, and vanilla until smooth.
3. Add the coconut flour and cocoa powder, mixing until there are no lumps. The batter will be thick.
4. Spread the batter evenly in the baking dish. Bake for 20-25 minutes, or until a toothpick inserted in the center comes out clean. Let cool before cutting into squares.

Nutritional Facts (Per Serving): Calories: 250 | Carbohydrates: 3g | Protein: 5g | Fat: 22g | Fiber: 4g | Sodium: 130mg | Sugars: 0g

Keto Strawberry Shortcake Cups

Prep: 15 minutes | **Chill:** 1 hour | **Serves:** 4

Ingredients:

For the Shortcake:
- 1 cup almond flour (120g)
- 2 tbsp melted butter (30g)
- 1 tbsp powdered low-carb sweetener (10g)

For the Topping:
- 1/2 cup heavy cream (120ml)
- 2 tbsp sliced strawberries (25g)
- 1/2 tsp vanilla extract (2.5ml)
- Low carb sweetener to taste

Instructions:

1. In a bowl, mix the almond flour, melted butter, and powdered sweetener until the mixture resembles a crumbly dough. Press this mixture evenly into the bottom of small serving cups to form a solid shortcake crust layer.
2. In a separate mixing bowl, add the heavy cream, vanilla extract, and a pinch of low-carb sweetener. Whip the cream until soft peaks form, creating a light and airy texture for the topping.
3. Spoon a generous layer of the whipped cream over each shortcake crust, then gently place sliced strawberries on top of the whipped cream.
4. Chill the shortcake cups in the refrigerator for at least 1 hour before serving. Serve cold.

Nutritional Facts (Per Serving): Calories: 250 | Carbohydrates: 2g | Protein: 4g | Fat: 23g | Fiber: 3g | Sodium: 120mg | Sugars: 0g

Keto Espresso Chocolate Torte

Prep: 15 minutes | **Cook:** 30 minutes | **Chill:** 1 hour | **Serves:** 4

Ingredients:

- 1/2 cup almond flour (60g)
- 1/4 cup cocoa powder (25g)
- 1/4 cup melted coconut oil (60ml)
- 2 large eggs
- 2 tbsp espresso powder (10g)
- 1/4 cup powdered low-carb sweetener (30g)
- 1/2 tsp vanilla extract (2.5ml)

Instructions:

1. Preheat your oven to 350°F (175°C) and grease a small round cake pan or line it with parchment paper to prevent sticking.
2. In a medium bowl, whisk together the almond flour, cocoa powder, and espresso powder.
3. In a separate bowl, combine the melted coconut oil, eggs, powdered sweetener, and vanilla extract, whisking until well-blended. Gradually fold the dry ingredients into the wet ingredients, and stir well.
4. Pour the batter into the prepared pan and smooth the top with a spatula. Bake for 25-30 minutes. Allow the torte to cool completely, then refrigerate for 1 hour to set before slicing. Serve chilled for a rich, decadent dessert.

Nutritional Facts (Per Serving): Calories: 250 | Carbohydrates: 3g | Protein: 5g | Fat: 23g | Fiber: 3g | Sodium: 130mg | Sugars: 0g

Keto Almond Butter Cookies

Prep: 10 minutes | Cook: 12 minutes | Serves: 4

Ingredients:

- 1/2 cup almond butter (120g)
- 1/4 cup powdered low-carb sweetener (30g)
- 1 large egg
- 1/2 tsp vanilla extract (2.5ml)
- 1/4 tsp baking powder (1g)

Instructions:

1. Preheat the oven to 350°F (175°C) and line a baking sheet with parchment paper.
2. In a mixing bowl, combine the almond butter, powdered sweetener, egg, vanilla extract, and baking powder. Stir until the ingredients form a smooth, thick dough with no visible lumps.
3. Using a tablespoon, scoop out portions of dough and roll them into small balls. Place each dough ball on the prepared baking sheet, leaving a bit of space between each. Flatten each ball gently with a fork to create a crisscross pattern on top.
4. Bake for 10-12 minutes, or until the edges are golden brown. Allow the cookies to cool on the baking sheet for 5 minutes before transferring them to a wire rack to cool completely.

Nutritional Facts (Per Serving): Calories: 250 | Carbohydrates: 3g | Protein: 6g | Fat: 22g | Fiber: 3g | Sodium: 125mg | Sugars: 0g

Elegant Keto Torte with Fresh Berries

Prep: 20 minutes | Cook: 25 minutes | Chill: 1 hour | Serves: 4

Ingredients:

For the Torte:
- 1 cup almond flour (120g)
- 1/4 cup cocoa powder (25g)
- 1/4 cup melted butter (60ml)
- 2 large eggs
- 1/4 cup powdered low-carb sweetener (30g)
- 1/2 tsp vanilla extract (2.5ml)

For the Topping:
- 1/4 cup mixed fresh berries (40g)
- 1 tbsp powdered low-carb sweetener (10g)

Instructions:

1. Preheat oven to 350°F (175°C) and grease a small cake pan. In a bowl, mix the almond flour, cocoa powder, melted butter, eggs, sweetener, and vanilla until smooth.
2. Pour the batter into the prepared pan, spreading evenly. Bake for 20-25 minutes. Cool completely.
3. Top the torte with fresh berries and a light dusting of sweetener. Refrigerate for 1 hour before serving to allow flavors to meld.
4. Serve chilled, with a few berries on the side.

Nutritional Facts (Per Serving): Calories: 250 | Carbohydrates: 2g | Protein: 6g | Fat: 22g | Fiber: 3g | Sodium: 130mg | Sugars: 0g

Decadent Keto Chocolate Ganache Tart

Prep: 20 minutes | Cook: 15 minutes | Chill: 1 hour | Serves: 4

Ingredients:

For the Crust:
- 1 cup almond flour (120g)
- 2 tbsp melted butter (30g)
- 1 tbsp powdered low-carb sweetener (10g)

For the Ganache Filling:
- 1/2 cup heavy cream (120ml)
- 1/2 cup dark chocolate, chopped (60g)
- 1/2 tsp vanilla extract (2.5ml)

Instructions:

1. Preheat oven to 350°F (175°C). In a bowl, mix almond flour, melted butter, and sweetener for the crust. Press into a tart pan to form an even layer.
2. Bake the crust for 8-10 minutes, until lightly golden. Remove from oven and let cool.
3. In a small saucepan, heat heavy cream over medium heat until just simmering. Remove from heat, add dark chocolate, and let sit for 1-2 minutes. Stir until chocolate is fully melted and smooth. Add vanilla extract.
4. Pour ganache into the cooled crust and refrigerate for 1 hour until set. Serve chilled for a rich, indulgent treat.

Nutritional Facts (Per Serving): Calories: 250 | Carbohydrates: 3g | Protein: 4g | Fat: 23g | Fiber: 2g | Sodium: 125mg | Sugars: 0g

Creamy Coconut Lime Cheesecake

Prep: 20 minutes | Chill: 2 hours | Serves: 4

Ingredients:

For the Filling:
- 1/2 cup cream cheese, softened (120g)
- 1/4 cup coconut cream (60ml)
- 1 tbsp lime juice (15ml)
- 1 tsp lime zest (5g)
- 1 tbsp powdered low-carb sweetener (10g)

For the Crust:
- 1/2 cup almond flour (60g)
- 2 tbsp melted coconut oil (30ml)
- 1 tbsp powdered low-carb sweetener (10g)

Instructions:

1. In a bowl, mix almond flour, melted coconut oil, and sweetener to create a crumbly crust. Press this mixture into the bottom of small serving cups.
2. In another bowl, beat the cream cheese, coconut cream, lime juice, lime zest, and sweetener until smooth and creamy.
3. Spoon the lime cheesecake filling over the crust in each cup, smoothing the tops.
4. Chill in the refrigerator for at least 2 hours to set. Garnish with extra lime zest if desired before serving.

Nutritional Facts (Per Serving): Calories: 250 | Carbohydrates: 3g | Protein: 5g | Fat: 23g | Fiber: 2g | Sodium: 120mg | Sugars: 0g

Lemon Ricotta Keto Pound Cake

Prep: 15 minutes | Cook: 45 minutes | Serves: 4

Ingredients:

- 1 cup almond flour (120g)
- 1/2 cup ricotta cheese (120g)
- 1/4 cup melted butter (60g)
- 3 large eggs
- 2 tbsp lemon juice (30ml)
- 1 tbsp lemon zest (5g)
- 1/4 cup powdered low-carb sweetener (30g)
- 1/2 tsp baking powder (2g)
- 1/2 tsp vanilla extract (2.5ml)

Instructions:

1. Preheat your oven to 350°F (175°C) and line a small loaf pan with parchment paper.
2. In a large mixing bowl, combine almond flour, baking powder, and sweetener.
3. In a separate bowl, whisk together the ricotta, melted butter, eggs, lemon juice, lemon zest, and vanilla extract until smooth and creamy.
4. Gradually add the wet ingredients to the dry ingredients, stirring gently until a thick batter forms.
5. Pour the batter into the prepared loaf pan. Bake for 40-45 minutes.
6. Allow the cake to cool in the pan for 10 minutes before transferring to a wire rack to cool completely.

Nutritional Facts (Per Serving): Calories: 250 | Carbohydrates: 3g | Protein: 7g | Fat: 22g | Fiber: 2g | Sodium: 125mg | Sugars: 0g

Matcha Green Tea Keto Cheesecake

Prep: 15 minutes | Cook: 50 minutes | Chill: 2 hours | Serves: 4

Ingredients:

For the Filling:
- 8 oz cream cheese, softened (225g)
- 1/4 cup coconut cream (60ml)
- 1 tbsp matcha powder (5g)
- 1/4 cup powdered low-carb sweetener (30g)
- 1 large egg
- 1/2 tsp vanilla extract (2.5ml)

For the Crust:
- 1 cup almond flour (120g)
- 2 tbsp melted butter (30g)
- 1 tbsp powdered low-carb sweetener (10g)

Instructions:

1. Preheat oven to 325°F (160°C). In a bowl, mix almond flour, melted butter, and sweetener. Press into the bottom of a small springform pan to form an even crust and bake for 8-10 minutes. Let cool.
2. In a mixing bowl, beat the cream cheese, coconut cream, matcha powder, sweetener, egg, and vanilla extract until smooth.
3. Pour the filling over the cooled crust. Bake for 40-50 minutes until the center is set.
4. Let the cheesecake cool, then refrigerate for 2 hours before serving. Dust with matcha powder.

Nutritional Facts (Per Serving): Calories: 250 | Carbohydrates: 3g | Protein: 5g | Fat: 23g | Fiber: 2g | Sodium: 130mg | Sugars: 0g

CHAPTER 15: DINNER: Keto Dinners in Minutes

Keto Broccoli Fritters with Cheese and Yogurt Sauce

Prep: 15 minutes | Cook: 20 minutes | Serves: 2

Ingredients:

- 1 1/2 cups broccoli florets, chopped (200g)
- 1 1/4 cups shredded cheddar cheese (125g)
- 2 large eggs (100g)
- 3 tbsp almond flour (22g)
- 1 1/4 tsp garlic powder (6g)
- 1 1/2 tbsp olive oil (22ml)
- Salt and pepper to taste
- For the Sauce:
- 1/3 cup full-fat unsweetened Greek yogurt (80g)
- 1 tbsp fresh dill, chopped (4g)

Instructions:

1. In a bowl, mix chopped broccoli, cheese, egg, almond flour, garlic powder, salt, and pepper. Form small fritters with the mixture.
2. Heat olive oil in a skillet over medium heat and cook fritters until golden, about 3-4 minutes per side.
3. Serve with Greek yogurt sauce, garnished with fresh dill.

Nutritional Facts (Per Serving): Calories: 580 | Sugars: 2g | Fat: 50g | Carbohydrates: 7g | Protein: 35g | Fiber: 6g | Sodium: 500mg

Keto Chicken Fajita Lettuce Wraps

Prep: 15 minutes | Cook: 15 minutes | Serves: 2

Ingredients:

- 1 1/2 tbsp olive oil (22ml)
- 10 oz chicken breast, thinly sliced (280g)
- 3/4 bell pepper, sliced (110g)
- 3/4 onion, sliced (90g)
- 1 1/2 tsp chili powder (7g)
- 3/4 tsp cumin (3g)
- 6 large lettuce leaves (60g)
- Salt and pepper to taste

Instructions:

1. Heat a skillet over medium heat and add olive oil. Add the sliced chicken breast to the skillet. Season with salt, pepper, chili powder, and cumin.
2. Cook the chicken for 5-6 minutes, stirring occasionally, until the pieces are cooked through.
3. Add the sliced bell pepper and onion to the skillet. Sauté for an additional 4-5 minutes.
4. Lay out the lettuce leaves on a plate. Divide the chicken and vegetable mixture among the lettuce leaves.

Nutritional Information (Per Serving): Calories: 590 | Sugars: 2g | Fat: 45g | Carbohydrates: 8g | Protein: 50g | Fiber: 7g | Sodium: 550mg

Cheesy Zucchini Pizza Boats

Prep: 10 minutes | Cook: 30 minutes | Serves: 2

Ingredients:

- 2 medium zucchinis, halved lengthwise, scooped (300g)
- 1 cup shredded mozzarella cheese (120g)
- 1/2 cup low-carb marinara sauce (120g)
- 1/3 cup sliced pepperoni (50g)
- 1/2 cup cooked ground beef (100g)
- 3/4 tsp Italian seasoning (3g)
- 1 1/2 tbsp olive oil (22ml)

Instructions:

1. Preheat the oven to 375°F (190°C). Brush zucchini halves with olive oil and place in a baking dish.
2. Spread a layer of low-carb marinara sauce over the zucchini. Arrange cooked ground beef evenly over the sauce.
3. Sprinkle half of the shredded mozzarella cheese over the beef, then top with pepperoni slices.
4. Add the remaining mozzarella cheese and sprinkle Italian seasoning over the zucchini.
5. Place the dish in the oven and bake for 25-30 minutes, or until the cheese is melted, bubbly, and slightly golden on top.
6. Let the pizza boats rest for a few minutes before serving to allow flavors to meld.

Nutritional Facts (Per Serving): Calories: 590 | Sugars: 3g | Fat: 48g | Carbohydrates: 9g | Protein: 42g | Fiber: 7g | Sodium: 600mg

Basil Pesto Chicken with Cherry Tomatoes

Prep: 10 minutes | Cook: 20 minutes | Serves: 2

Ingredients:

- 1 1/2 tbsp olive oil (22ml)
- 10 oz chicken breast, sliced (280g)
- 1/3 cup low-carb basil pesto (80g)
- 3/4 cup cherry tomatoes, halved (120g)
- Salt and pepper to taste

Instructions:

1. In a skillet, heat olive oil over medium heat. Add the sliced chicken breast, season with salt and pepper, and cook for 5-6 minutes, stirring occasionally, until the chicken is browned and cooked through.
2. Add the basil pesto to the skillet, stirring to coat the chicken pieces evenly.
3. Once the chicken is coated, add the halved cherry tomatoes to the skillet. Cook for another 3-4 minutes, just until the tomatoes begin to soften and release their juices.
4. Serve hot, with the tomatoes arranged around the chicken for a burst of color and flavor.

Nutritional Facts (Per Serving): Calories: 580 | Sugars: 2g | Fat: 50g | Carbohydrates: 8g | Protein: 45g | Fiber: 6g | Sodium: 500mg

Crispy Pork Chops with Cabbage Slaw

Prep: 15 minutes | Cook: 20 minutes | Serves: 2

Ingredients:

- 2 pork chops, bone-in (250g each)
- 2/3 cup almond flour (80g)
- 1/3 cup grated Parmesan cheese (40g)
- 1 large egg, beaten (50g)
- Salt and pepper to taste
- 1 1/2 tbsp olive oil (22ml)
- For the Slaw:
- 2 1/2 cups shredded cabbage (180g)
- 1/3 cup shredded carrots (40g)
- 2 tbsp apple cider vinegar (30g)
- 1 1/2 tbsp olive oil (22ml)

Instructions:

1. In a shallow bowl, combine almond flour, Parmesan cheese, salt, and pepper.
2. Dip each pork chop in beaten egg, then coat with the almond flour mixture, pressing gently to adhere.
3. Heat olive oil in a skillet over medium-high heat. Cook the pork chops for 5-6 minutes per side until golden and crispy.
4. In a bowl, combine shredded cabbage, carrots, apple cider vinegar, and olive oil. Toss well.
5. Serve the pork chops alongside the cabbage slaw.

Nutritional Facts (Per Serving): Calories: 590 | Sugars: 3g | Fat: 48g | Carbohydrates: 8g | Protein: 42g | Fiber: 7g | Sodium: 580mg

Balsamic Steak Bites with Asparagus Spears

Prep: 10 minutes | Cook: 15 minutes | Serves: 2

Ingredients:

- 10 oz sirloin steak, cubed (280g)
- Salt and pepper to taste
- 1 1/2 tbsp low-carb balsamic vinegar (22ml)
- 1 1/2 tbsp olive oil (22ml)
- 2/3 lb asparagus spears, trimmed (300g)
- 2 cloves garlic, minced (6g)

Instructions:

1. Season the steak cubes generously with salt and pepper. In a large skillet, heat olive oil over medium-high heat until shimmering.
2. Add the steak to the skillet in a single layer, searing each side for 4-5 minutes until browned and cooked to desired doneness. Drizzle balsamic vinegar over the steak and cook for an additional minute, stirring to coat and caramelize the meat.
3. Remove the steak and set aside. Add the minced garlic to the skillet, followed by the asparagus spears, and sauté for about 3-4 minutes until the asparagus is bright green and tender-crisp.
4. Serve the steak bites alongside the asparagus spears for a simple, flavorful dish.

Nutritional Facts (Per Serving): Calories: 600 | Sugars: 2g | Fat: 50g | Carbohydrates: 7g | Protein: 48g | Fiber: 6g | Sodium: 450mg

Keto Chicken Piccata with Zoodles

Prep: 10 minutes | Cook: 15 minutes | Serves: 2

Ingredients:

- 10 oz chicken breast, thinly sliced (280g)
- Salt and pepper to taste
- 1 1/2 tbsp almond flour (10g)
- 1/3 cup low-sodium and sugar-free chicken broth (80g)
- 1 1/2 tbsp olive oil (22ml)
- 3 tbsp lemon juice (45g)
- 1 1/2 tbsp capers (15g)
- 1 1/2 tbsp unsalted butter (22g)
- 2 1/2 cups zucchini noodles (180g)

Instructions:

1. Season the chicken slices on both sides with salt and pepper, then lightly dust each slice with almond flour to create a thin, crispy coating.
2. In a skillet, heat the olive oil over medium heat. Add the chicken slices and cook for 3-4 minutes on each side until golden brown and cooked through. Remove from the skillet and set aside.
3. In the same skillet, add chicken broth, lemon juice, capers, and butter. Stir well, scraping up any browned bits, and let the sauce simmer for 2-3 minutes until it thickens slightly.
4. Add the zucchini noodles to the skillet and toss gently, cooking until they're just tender, about 2 minutes. Serve the chicken over the zoodles, with the lemon-caper sauce drizzled on top.

Nutritional Facts (Per Serving): Calories: 590 | Sugars: 1g | Fat: 50g | Carbohydrates: 7g | Protein: 40g | Fiber: 6g | Sodium: 500mg

Herbed Turkey Meatballs with Marinara Sauce

Prep: 10 minutes | Cook: 25 minutes | Serves: 2

Ingredients:

- 10 oz ground turkey (280g)
- 1/3 cup almond flour (40g)
- 1/3 cup grated Parmesan cheese (40g)
- 1 large egg (50g)
- 1 1/4 tsp dried Italian herbs (6g)
- Salt and pepper to taste
- 1 1/2 tbsp olive oil (22ml)
- 3/4 cup low-carb marinara sauce (180g)

Instructions:

1. In a mixing bowl, combine the ground turkey, almond flour, Parmesan, egg, Italian herbs, salt, and pepper. Mix well, then shape into small meatballs, about 1 inch in diameter.
2. In a skillet, heat olive oil over medium heat. Place the meatballs in the skillet in a single layer. Brown the meatballs on all sides, turning occasionally, for about 10 minutes until golden.
3. Pour the marinara sauce over the meatballs, reduce the heat to low, and cover. Simmer for an additional 10 minutes.
4. Serve the meatballs hot with marinara sauce spooned over them, garnished with fresh herbs.

Nutritional Facts (Per Serving): Calories: 590 | Sugars: 2g | Fat: 48g | Carbohydrates: 8g | Protein: 45g | Fiber: 7g | Sodium: 550mg

CHAPTER 16: DINNER: Filling Salads

Grilled Chicken Caesar Salad with Parmesan Crisps

Prep: 15 minutes | Cook: 20 minutes | Serves: 2

Ingredients:

- 10 oz chicken breast, boneless and skinless (280g)
- Salt and pepper to taste
- 1 1/2 tbsp olive oil (22ml)
- 5 cups romaine lettuce, chopped (250g)
- 1/3 cup low-carb Caesar dressing (80g)
- 1/3 cup grated Parmesan cheese (40g)
- For Parmesan Crisps:
- 1/3 cup shredded Parmesan cheese (40g)

Instructions:

1. Preheat grill to medium-high heat. Season the chicken breast with salt, pepper, and olive oil.
2. Grill the chicken for about 5-6 minutes per side. Let rest for a few minutes, then slice thinly.
3. Preheat the oven to 400°F (200°C). Place small mounds of shredded Parmesan on a baking sheet lined with parchment paper. Bake for 5-7 minutes.
4. Toss the chopped romaine lettuce with Caesar dressing. Top with sliced grilled chicken and Parmesan crisps.

Nutritional Facts (Per Serving): Calories: 580 | Sugars: 1g | Fat: 48g | Carbohydrates: 7g | Protein: 45g | Fiber: 6g | Sodium: 600mg

Keto Nicoise Salad with Hard-Boiled Eggs

Prep: 15 minutes | Cook: 10 minutes | Serves: 2

Ingredients:

- 3/4 cup cherry tomatoes, halved (120g)
- 3/4 cup green beans, blanched (110g)
- 5 oz canned tuna in olive oil, drained (140g)
- 2 large eggs, hard-boiled and halved (100g)
- 5 cups mixed greens (250g)
- 1/3 cup low-sodium black olives (50g)
- 3 tbsp extra-virgin olive oil (45ml)
- 1 1/2 tbsp red wine vinegar (22ml)

Instructions:

1. Arrange mixed greens on a large plate. Distribute the halved cherry tomatoes, blanched green beans, and black olives evenly across the greens.
2. Break the tuna into chunks and place it on the salad, followed by the halved hard-boiled eggs.
3. In a small bowl, whisk together olive oil, red wine vinegar, salt, and pepper to make the dressing. Drizzle the dressing evenly over the salad.
4. Serve immediately, garnishing with fresh herbs.

Nutritional Facts (Per Serving): Calories: 590 | Sugars: 1g | Fat: 50g | Carbohydrates: 7g | Protein: 42g | Fiber: 6g | Sodium: 600mg

Greek Salad with Grilled Lamb

Prep: 15 minutes | Cook: 15 minutes | Serves: 2

Ingredients:

- 8 oz lamb loin, trimmed and cut into cubes (225g)
- Salt and pepper to taste
- 1 1/2 tbsp olive oil (22ml)
- 3/4 cup cucumber, diced (110g)
- 3/4 cup cherry tomatoes, halved (120g)
- 1/3 cup red onion, thinly sliced (40g)
- 1/3 cup Kalamata olives (50g)
- 1/3 cup low-sodium feta cheese, crumbled (40g)
- 5 cups romaine lettuce, chopped (250g)
- 1 1/2 tbsp red wine vinegar (22ml)

Instructions:

1. Preheat grill to medium-high heat. Season lamb cubes with salt, pepper, and olive oil.
2. Grill lamb for about 2-3 minutes per side or until desired doneness. Let the lamb rest for a few minutes, then set aside.
3. In a large bowl, combine cucumber, cherry tomatoes, red onion, olives, and romaine lettuce.
4. Drizzle red wine vinegar over the salad and toss to coat. Top with grilled lamb cubes and sprinkle with crumbled feta.

Nutritional Facts (Per Serving): Calories: 580 | Sugars: 2g | Fat: 48g | Carbohydrates: 7g | Protein: 45g | Fiber: 6g | Sodium: 550mg

Steak Salad with Spinach, Walnuts, and Balsamic

Prep: 10 minutes | Cook: 10 minutes | Serves: 2

Ingredients:

- 10 oz sirloin steak, cooked to preference (280g)
- Salt and pepper to taste
- 1 1/2 tbsp olive oil (22ml)
- 5 cups baby spinach (150g)
- 1/3 cup walnuts, toasted (40g)
- 1/3 cup crumbled blue cheese (40g)
- 3/4 cup cherry tomatoes, halved (120g)
- 1 1/2 tbsp low-carb balsamic vinegar (22ml)

Instructions:

1. Season steak with salt and pepper. Heat olive oil in a skillet over medium-high heat and cook steak for 4-5 minutes per side, or until cooked to desired doneness. Let the steak rest for a few minutes, then slice thinly.
2. In a large bowl, combine baby spinach, toasted walnuts, crumbled blue cheese, and cherry tomatoes.
3. Drizzle balsamic vinegar over the salad and toss gently. Arrange the sliced steak on top of the salad. Serve immediately, adding extra cracked black pepper if desired.

Nutritional Facts (Per Serving): Calories: 590 | Sugars: 2g | Fat: 50g | Carbohydrates: 8g | Protein: 47g | Fiber: 6g | Sodium: 550mg

Crispy Chicken and Avocado Salad

Prep: 15 minutes | Cook: 20 minutes | Serves: 2

Ingredients:

- 10 oz chicken breast, thinly sliced (280g)
- Salt and pepper to taste
- 1/3 cup almond flour (40g)
- 1/3 cup grated Parmesan cheese (40g)
- 1 large egg, beaten (50g)
- 1 1/2 tbsp olive oil (22ml)
- 1 1/2 tbsp lemon juice (22ml)
- 5 cups mixed greens (250g)
- 3/4 avocado, sliced (100g)
- 1/3 cup cucumber, diced (60g)
- 1/3 cup cherry tomatoes, halved (50g)
- 1 1/2 tbsp olive oil (22ml)

Instructions:

1. In a shallow bowl, combine almond flour, Parmesan cheese, salt, and pepper. Dip each chicken slice into the beaten egg, then coat with the almond flour mixture, pressing gently to adhere.
2. In a skillet, heat olive oil over medium heat. Cook the coated chicken for 4-5 minutes per side. Remove from skillet and cool slightly before slicing.
3. In a large bowl, toss mixed greens with cucumber, cherry tomatoes, and avocado slices.
4. In a small bowl, whisk together olive oil and lemon juice, then drizzle over the salad. Arrange the crispy chicken slices on top.

Nutritional Facts (Per Serving): Calories: 590 | Sugars: 2g | Fat: 50g | Carbohydrates: 8g | Protein: 45g | Fiber: 7g | Sodium: 500mg

Bunless Steakhouse Salad

Prep: 10 minutes | Cook: 10 minutes | Serves: 2

Ingredients:

- 10 oz ribeye steak, cooked to preference (280g)
- Salt and pepper to taste
- 1 1/2 tbsp olive oil (22ml)
- 5 cups romaine lettuce, chopped (250g)
- 3/4 cup cherry tomatoes, halved (120g)
- 1/3 cup red onion, thinly sliced (40g)
- 1/3 cup blue cheese crumbles (40g)
- 1/3 cup sliced cucumber (60g)
- 1 1/2 tbsp balsamic vinegar (22ml)

Instructions:

1. Season steak with salt and pepper. In a skillet over medium-high heat, add olive oil and cook the steak for 4-5 minutes per side, or until desired doneness. Remove from the skillet and let rest for a few minutes before slicing thinly.
2. In a large salad bowl, combine romaine lettuce, cherry tomatoes, red onion, blue cheese crumbles, and cucumber slices.
3. Drizzle balsamic vinegar over the salad and toss gently to coat. Arrange the sliced steak on top.
4. Serve immediately with additional black pepper if desired.

Nutritional Facts (Per Serving): Calories: 590 | Sugars: 2g | Fat: 52g | Carbohydrates: 7g | Protein: 45g | Fiber: 6g | Sodium: 550mg

CHAPTER 17: DINNER: Keto Vegan: Fresh Flavors

Vegan Mushroom Stroganoff with Shirataki Noodles

Prep: 10 minutes | **Cook:** 20 minutes | **Serves:** 2

Ingredients:

- 1 1/2 tbsp olive oil (22ml)
- 1 small onion, diced (90g)
- 2 cloves garlic, minced (6g)
- 10 oz cremini mushrooms, sliced (280g)
- Salt and pepper to taste
- 2/3 cup unsweetened coconut milk, full-fat (160g)
- 1 1/2 tbsp Dijon mustard (22g)
- 1 1/2 tbsp tamari or soy sauce (22g)
- 1/3 cup vegetable broth (80g)
- 1 1/2 packages shirataki noodles, drained and rinsed (300g)
- Fresh parsley, chopped, for garnish

Instructions:

1. Sauté onion and garlic in olive oil over medium heat until softened. Add mushrooms, salt, and pepper, cooking until golden.
2. Stir in coconut milk, Dijon mustard, tamari, and vegetable broth; simmer until thickened.
3. Add shirataki noodles and cook for 2-3 minutes.
4. Serve garnished with fresh parsley.

Nutritional Facts (Per Serving): Calories: 590 | Sugars: 2g | Fat: 50g | Carbohydrates: 8g | Protein: 12g | Fiber: 7g | Sodium: 550mg

Eggplant Caponata with Olives and Fresh Herbs

Prep: 15 minutes | **Cook:** 25 minutes | **Serves:** 2

Ingredients:

- 1 1/2 tbsp olive oil (22ml)
- 1 large eggplant, diced (250g)
- 3/4 red bell pepper, diced (110g)
- 1/3 cup red onion, diced (40g)
- 3 tbsp tomato paste (45g)
- 1/3 cup Kalamata olives, chopped (50g)
- 1 1/2 tbsp capers, rinsed (15g)
- Salt and pepper to taste
- 1 1/2 tbsp sugar-free red wine vinegar (22ml)
- Fresh basil and parsley, chopped, for garnish

Instructions:

1. Heat olive oil in a skillet, then cook eggplant, bell pepper, and onion until softened.
2. Add tomato paste, olives, and capers, cooking for a few more minutes. Season with salt, pepper, and red wine vinegar.
3. Serve warm or at room temperature, garnished with fresh herbs.

Nutritional Facts (Per Serving): Calories: 590 | Sugars: 3g | Fat: 50g | Carbohydrates: 9g | Protein: 8g | Fiber: 8g | Sodium: 500mg

Cauliflower Steak with Herb Sauce

Prep: 10 minutes | Cook: 25 minutes | Serves: 2

Ingredients:

- 2 large cauliflower steaks, cut thick (400g total)
- 3 tbsp olive oil (45ml), divided
- 1/4 cup pine nuts, toasted (30g)
- 2 tbsp capers, rinsed and chopped (20g)
- 2 tbsp fresh parsley, chopped (10g)
- 1 tbsp fresh rosemary, chopped (5g)
- 2 tbsp lemon juice (30ml)
- Salt and pepper to taste

Instructions:

1. Preheat oven to 400°F (200°C). Arrange cauliflower steaks on a baking sheet, brushing each side with 1 tbsp of olive oil and seasoning with salt and pepper.
2. Roast cauliflower for 20-25 minutes, flipping halfway through, until edges are golden and cauliflower is tender.
3. While cauliflower is roasting, prepare the herb sauce by mixing parsley, rosemary, lemon juice, capers, and the remaining olive oil in a small bowl.
4. Once cauliflower steaks are done, drizzle with the herb sauce and serve immediately.

Nutritional Facts (Per Serving): Calories: 520 | Sugars: 3g | Fat: 48g | Carbohydrates: 10g | Protein: 9g | Fiber: 6g | Sodium: 500mg

One-Pan Keto Ratatouille with Bacon

Prep: 10 minutes | Cook: 25 minutes | Serves: 2

Ingredients:

- 4 slices bacon, diced (60g)
- 2 cups cauliflower florets (200g)
- 1 cup zucchini, diced (150g)
- 1/2 cup red bell pepper, diced (75g)
- 1 cup eggplant, diced (120g)
- 1/2 cup cherry tomatoes, halved (80g)
- 2 tbsp olive oil (30ml)
- 1 tsp Italian seasoning (5g)
- Salt and pepper to taste
- Fresh basil, chopped, for garnish

Instructions:

1. In a large skillet, cook the bacon over medium heat until crispy, about 5 minutes. Remove bacon from the skillet and set aside.
2. Add the zucchini, red bell pepper, eggplant, and cherry tomatoes to the skillet with bacon fat. Season with salt, pepper, and Italian seasoning.
3. Sauté the vegetables for 10-12 minutes until tender and lightly browned, stirring occasionally.
4. Return the bacon to the skillet, tossing everything together, and cook for an additional 2-3 minutes to heat through.
5. Serve garnished with fresh basil.

Nutritional Facts (Per Serving): Calories: 580 | Sugars: 4g | Fat: 50g | Carbohydrates: 10g | Protein: 12g | Fiber: 7g | Sodium: 550mg

CHAPTER 18: DINNER: Taste of the Sea

Spanish-Inspired Seafood Medley with Saffron Cauliflower Rice

Prep: 15 minutes | Cook: 20 minutes | Serves: 2

Ingredients:

- 1 1/2 tbsp olive oil (22ml)
- 1/2 small onion, diced (60g)
- 2 cloves garlic, minced (6g)
- 2 1/2 cups cauliflower rice (250g)
- 1/2 tsp saffron threads, soaked in 2 tbsp warm water (10g)
- 3/4 cup seafood or vegetable broth (180ml)
- 5 oz shrimp, peeled and deveined (140g)
- 5 oz white fish, cubed (140g)
- 6 mussels, cleaned and debearded (100g)
- Salt and pepper to taste
- Fresh parsley, chopped, for garnish

Instructions:

1. Heat olive oil in a large skillet over medium heat. Sauté onion and garlic about 3-4 minutes.
2. Add cauliflower rice, saffron water, and broth to the skillet. Let cook for 5 minutes.
3. Add shrimp, white fish, and mussels. Season with salt and pepper, cover. Cook for 6-8 minutes.
4. Serve hot, garnished with fresh parsley.

Nutritional Facts (Per Serving): Calories: 580 | Sugars: 2g | Fat: 45g | Carbohydrates: 7g | Protein: 45g | Fiber: 6g | Sodium: 550mg

Mediterranean Baked Sardines with Olive Oil and Fennel Salad

Prep: 10 minutes | Cook: 20 minutes | Serves: 2

Ingredients:

- 6 whole sardines, cleaned (300g)
- Salt and pepper to taste
- 2 tbsp olive oil, divided (30g)
- 1/2 lemon, sliced (40g)
- 1 small fennel bulb, thinly sliced (80g)
- 1 tbsp lemon juice (15g)
- Fresh parsley and dill, chopped, for garnish

Instructions:

1. Preheat oven to 400°F (200°C). Arrange sardines on a baking sheet, season with salt, pepper, and 1 tbsp olive oil, and layer lemon slices on top.
2. Bake for 15-20 minutes until sardines are cooked through and crispy.
3. Meanwhile, toss fennel slices with remaining olive oil, lemon juice, salt, and pepper. Serve baked sardines with fennel salad on the side, garnished with parsley and dill.

Nutritional Facts (Per Serving): Calories: 500 | Sugars: 1g | Fat: 40g | Carbohydrates: 5g | Protein: 30g | Fiber: 6g | Sodium: 480mg

Grilled Mackerel with Caper & Lemon Dressing

Prep: 15 minutes | Cook: 25 minutes | Serves: 2

Ingredients:

- 2 whole mackerel, cleaned and gutted (350g)
- Salt and pepper to taste
- 2 tbsp olive oil, divided (30ml)
- 1 tbsp capers, rinsed and chopped (10g)
- 1 tbsp lemon juice (15ml)
- 1 tbsp fresh parsley, chopped (5g)
- 1 tsp Dijon mustard (5g)
- 1 clove garlic, minced (3g)

Instructions:

1. Preheat grill to medium-high heat. Season mackerel inside and out with salt and pepper. Brush with 1 tbsp olive oil.
2. Grill mackerel for 6-8 minutes per side, until the skin is crispy and the flesh is cooked through.
3. Meanwhile, prepare the dressing by whisking together remaining olive oil, capers, lemon juice,
4. Dijon mustard, garlic, and parsley.
5. Drizzle caper & lemon dressing over the grilled mackerel and serve hot.

Nutritional Facts (Per Serving): Calories: 560 | Sugars: 1g | Fat: 45g | Carbohydrates: 3g | Protein: 40g | Fiber: 1g | Sodium: 500mg

Herb Butter Shrimp with Creamy Cauliflower Gruyère Mash

Prep: 10 minutes | Cook: 20 minutes | Serves: 2

Ingredients:

- 1 1/2 tbsp butter (22g)
- 1 tbsp olive oil (15ml)
- 9 oz shrimp, peeled and deveined (255g)
- Salt and pepper to taste
- 1/2 tsp garlic powder (2g)
- 2 1/2 cups steamed cauliflower (250g)
- 1/3 cup Gruyère cheese, grated (40g)
- 3 tbsp heavy cream (45ml)

Instructions:

1. In a skillet, melt butter and add olive oil over medium heat. Season the shrimp with salt, pepper, and garlic powder, then add to the skillet. Cook for 3-4 minutes, stirring occasionally, until shrimp are pink and cooked through. Remove shrimp from the skillet and set aside, keeping warm.
2. For the cauliflower mash, place steamed cauliflower in a blender or food processor. Add Gruyere cheese and heavy cream, blending until smooth and creamy. Taste and adjust seasoning with salt and pepper as needed.
3. Serve the herb butter shrimp over the creamy cauliflower mash. Garnish with fresh parsley.

Nutritional Facts (Per Serving): Calories: 590 | Sugars: 1g | Fat: 50g | Carbohydrates: 5g | Protein: 42g | Fiber: 3g | Sodium: 520mg

Baked Mackerel in Tomato Sauce with Asparagus

Prep: 10 minutes | Cook: 25 minutes | Serves: 2

Ingredients:

- 2 whole mackerel, cleaned (450g)
- 1 1/2 tbsp olive oil (22ml)
- Salt and pepper to taste
- 1 1/4 cups canned crushed tomatoes (300g)
- 1/2 small onion, diced (60g)
- 2 cloves garlic, minced (6g)
- 1 tsp smoked paprika (5g)
- 1/2 lb asparagus, trimmed (225g)

Instructions:

1. Preheat oven to 375°F (190°C). Season the mackerel with salt and pepper, then drizzle with olive oil. Place in a baking dish.
2. In a skillet, heat a small amount of olive oil over medium heat. Sauté the onion and garlic until softened, about 3-4 minutes. Add the crushed tomatoes, smoked paprika, salt, and pepper. Simmer for 5 minutes.
3. Pour the tomato sauce over the mackerel. Arrange the asparagus around the fish.
4. Bake for 20-25 minutes until the mackerel is cooked through, and the asparagus is tender.
5. Serve warm, spooning the tomato sauce over the fish and asparagus.

Nutritional Facts (Per Serving): Calories: 560 | Sugars: 3g | Fat: 45g | Carbohydrates: 7g | Protein: 38g | Fiber: 6g | Sodium: 500mg

Pesto-Crusted Salmon with Red Cabbage and Kale Salad

Prep: 10 minutes | Cook: 20 minutes | Serves: 2

Ingredients:

- 2 salmon fillets (170g each)
- 3 tbsp basil pesto (45g)
- 1 tbsp almond flour (7g)
- 1 tbsp olive oil (15ml)
- Salt and pepper to taste
- For the salad:
- 2 1/2 cups red cabbage, thinly sliced (180g)
- 1 cup kale, chopped (60g)
- 1 1/2 tbsp lemon juice (22ml)
- 1 1/2 tbsp olive oil (22ml)
- Salt and pepper to taste

Instructions:

1. Preheat oven to 400°F (200°C). Pat the salmon fillets dry and season with salt and pepper. Spread basil pesto evenly over the top of each fillet, then sprinkle with almond flour.
2. Place the salmon on a lined baking sheet and drizzle with olive oil. Bake for 12-15 minutes until the salmon is cooked through, and the crust is golden.
3. Meanwhile, prepare the salad. In a large bowl, toss red cabbage and kale with lemon juice, olive oil, salt, and pepper. Massage the kale lightly with your hands to soften.
4. Serve the salmon alongside the red cabbage and kale salad.

Nutritional Facts (Per Serving): Calories: 580 | Sugars: 2g | Fat: 50g | Carbohydrates: 7g | Protein: 36g | Fiber: 7g | Sodium: 480mg

Baked Cod with Olive Tapenade & Roasted Cherry Tomatoes

Prep: 10 minutes | **Cook:** 25 minutes | **Serves:** 2

Ingredients:

- 2 cod fillets (180g each)
- 1 tbsp olive oil (15ml)
- Salt and pepper to taste
- 1/2 cup black olives, pitted and chopped (75g)
- 1 tbsp capers, rinsed (10g)
- 1 tbsp lemon juice (15ml)
- 1 tbsp fresh parsley, chopped (5g)
- 1 cup cherry tomatoes, halved (160g)

Instructions:

1. Preheat oven to 375°F (190°C). Season cod fillets with salt and pepper, then drizzle with olive oil.
2. In a bowl, mix chopped olives, capers, lemon juice, and parsley to create the tapenade.
3. Arrange cod fillets on a baking sheet, spreading the tapenade evenly over the top. Scatter cherry tomatoes around the fish.
4. Bake for 20-25 minutes until the cod is opaque and flakes easily with a fork.
5. Serve warm, spooning roasted cherry tomatoes over the cod fillets.

Nutritional Facts (Per Serving): Calories: 550 | Sugars: 2g | Fat: 45g | Carbohydrates: 6g | Protein: 40g | Fiber: 5g | Sodium: 500mg

Seared Tuna Steaks with Avocado Salsa

Prep: 10 minutes | **Cook:** 20 minutes | **Serves:** 2

Ingredients:

- 2 tuna steaks (180g each)
- 1 tbsp olive oil (15ml)
- Salt and pepper to taste
- 1/2 tsp smoked paprika (2g)
- For the avocado salsa:
- 1/2 avocado, diced (75g)
- 1/4 cup cherry tomatoes, diced (40g)
- 1 tbsp red onion, finely chopped (10g)
- 1 tbsp fresh cilantro, chopped (5g)
- 1 tbsp lime juice (15ml)
- Salt and pepper to taste

Instructions:

1. Heat olive oil in a skillet over medium-high heat. Season tuna steaks with salt, pepper, and smoked paprika.
2. Sear tuna steaks for 2 minutes per side for a medium-rare texture or longer if desired. Remove from heat and let rest.
3. In a bowl, mix avocado, cherry tomatoes, red onion, cilantro, lime juice, salt, and pepper to prepare the salsa.
4. Serve the seared tuna steaks topped with avocado salsa.

Nutritional Facts (Per Serving): Calories: 570 | Sugars: 1g | Fat: 48g | Carbohydrates: 5g | Protein: 42g | Fiber: 4g | Sodium: 480mg

CHAPTER 19: DINNER: Family-Style Favorites

Garlic Grana Padano Chicken Wings

Prep: 10 minutes | Cook: 30 minutes | Serves: 2

Ingredients:

- 1 lb chicken wings (450g)
- 1 1/2 tbsp olive oil (22ml)
- 1/2 tsp smoked paprika (2g)
- 2 cloves garlic, minced (6g)
- Salt and pepper to taste
- 1/3 cup Grana Padano cheese, grated (40g)
- Fresh parsley, chopped, for garnish

Instructions:

1. Preheat oven to 400°F (200°C). Toss chicken wings with olive oil, smoked paprika, garlic, salt, and pepper in a large bowl until evenly coated.
2. Arrange wings on a baking sheet lined with parchment paper. Bake for 25-30 minutes, flipping halfway, until golden and crispy.
3. Remove wings from the oven and sprinkle with grated Grana Padano while still hot. Garnish with parsley before serving.

Nutritional Facts (Per Serving): Calories: 560 | Sugars: 0g | Fat: 45g | Carbohydrates: 2g | Protein: 39g | Fiber: 0g | Sodium: 480mg

Braised Pork Shank with Cabbage and Berry Sauce

Prep: 15 minutes | Cook: 2 hours | Serves: 2

Ingredients:

- 2 small pork shanks (total 1.5 lbs) (680g)
- Salt and pepper to taste
- 1 tbsp olive oil (15ml)
- 1/2 small onion, diced (50g)
- 1/2 head green cabbage, shredded (220g)
- 2 cloves garlic, minced (6g)
- 3/4 cup chicken broth, low sodium (180ml)
- 1/4 cup raspberries or blackberries, fresh or frozen (60g)
- 1 tbsp balsamic vinegar (15ml)
- 1 tbsp butter (for sauce) (15g)

Instructions:

1. Season pork shanks with salt and pepper. Heat olive oil in a large Dutch oven over medium heat and sear the shanks on all sides. Set aside.
2. Add onion and garlic to the pot. Stir in cabbage and cook for 3-4 minutes. Return the shanks to the pot, pour in the chicken broth, and braise over low heat for 1.5-2 hours, until the meat is tender.
3. In a small saucepan, simmer berries and balsamic vinegar. Serve pork shanks with cabbage and drizzle berry sauce on top.

Nutritional Facts (Per Serving): Calories: 580 | Sugars: 2g | Fat: 48g | Carbohydrates: 5g | Protein: 40g | Fiber: 6g | Sodium: 500mg

Baked Pork Ribs with Green Beans and Zucchini

Prep: 15 minutes | **Cook:** 45 minutes | **Serves:** 2

Ingredients:

- 1 lb pork ribs (450g)
- 1 1/2 tbsp olive oil (22ml)
- 1 tsp smoked paprika (5g)
- 1 tsp garlic powder (5g)
- Salt and pepper to taste
- 1 1/4 cups green beans, trimmed (180g)
- 1 cup zucchini, sliced (150g)
- 1 tbsp butter (for vegetables) (15g)

Instructions:

1. Preheat oven to 375°F (190°C). In a small bowl, mix olive oil, smoked paprika, garlic powder, salt, and pepper. Rub this marinade all over the pork ribs.
2. Place the ribs on a baking tray lined with foil. Cover with another piece of foil and bake for 35 minutes. Remove the top foil and bake for an additional 10 minutes to crisp up.
3. While ribs bake, steam green beans and zucchini until tender. Season lightly with salt and pepper.
4. Serve the ribs alongside the green beans and zucchini.

Nutritional Facts (Per Serving): Calories: 570 | Sugars: 1g | Fat: 47g | Carbohydrates: 6g | Protein: 38g | Fiber: 6g | Sodium: 480mg

Keto Beef Wellington with Baby Bella

Prep: 20 minutes | **Cook:** 30 minutes | **Serves:** 2

Ingredients:

- 8 oz beef tenderloin (225g)
- Salt and pepper to taste
- 2 tbsp olive oil (30g)
- 1 1/4 cups baby Bella mushrooms, finely chopped (180g)
- 1 clove garlic, minced (3g)
- 1 tbsp fresh parsley, chopped (5g)
- 1/3 cup almond flour (40g)
- 1 tbsp butter, melted (for brushing) (15g)
- 1 sheet low-carb pastry or almond-flour-based wrap (100g)

Instructions:

1. Preheat oven to 400°F (200°C). Season beef tenderloin with salt and pepper. Sear in a skillet with olive oil over high heat for 2 minutes on each side. Let cool.
2. In the same skillet, sauté mushrooms and garlic until liquid evaporates. Stir in parsley and set aside.
3. Roll out the pastry, spread the mushroom mixture over the center, and place the beef on top. Fold the pastry over the beef, sealing the edges.
4. Brush the pastry with melted butter and bake for 15-20 minutes until beef is medium-rare.
5. Rest for 5 minutes before slicing and serving.

Nutritional Facts (Per Serving): Calories: 590 | Sugars: 1g | Fat: 48g | Carbohydrates: 6g | Protein: 38g | Fiber: 5g | Sodium: 470mg

Creamy Tuscan Turkey Skillet with Sun-Dried Tomatoes & Spinach

Prep: 15 minutes | Cook: 45 minutes | Serves: 2

Ingredients:

- 8 oz ground turkey (225g)
- 1 tbsp olive oil (15g)
- 1/2 cup heavy cream (120ml)
- 1/4 cup sun-dried tomatoes, chopped (40g)
- 2 cups fresh spinach (60g)
- 1/4 cup grated Parmesan cheese (30g)
- 1/2 tsp garlic powder (2g)
- Salt and pepper to taste

Instructions:

1. Heat olive oil in a skillet over medium heat. Add ground turkey, breaking it up with a spatula, and cook for 6-7 minutes until browned.
2. Stir in sun-dried tomatoes, garlic powder, salt, and pepper. Cook for 1 minute.
3. Reduce heat to low, add heavy cream and spinach, and simmer for 2-3 minutes, stirring occasionally.
4. Stir in grated Parmesan and let the sauce thicken for another 2 minutes.
5. Serve warm, garnished with extra Parmesan or fresh basil.

Nutritional Facts (Per Serving): Calories: 540 | Sugars: 2g | Fat: 44g | Carbohydrates: 6g | Protein: 34g | Fiber: 6g | Sodium: 480mg

Roasted Duck Breast with Garlic Herb Butter & Sautéed Green Beans

Prep: 20 minutes | Cook: 30 minutes | Serves: 2

Ingredients:

- 2 duck breasts, skin-on (200g each)
- 1 tbsp olive oil (15g)
- 1/2 tsp salt (2g)
- 1/2 tsp black pepper (2g)
- 1 tbsp butter, melted (15g)
- 1 tsp fresh thyme, chopped (3g)
- 2 cloves garlic, minced (6g)
- For the Green Beans:
- 1 1/4 cups green beans, trimmed (180g)
- 1 tbsp butter (15g)
- 1/2 tsp garlic powder (2g)
- Salt and pepper to taste

Instructions:

1. Preheat oven to 375°F (190°C). Score the duck skin, season with salt and pepper.
2. Place skin-side down in a cold skillet over medium heat, cook 6-7 minutes, flip, and sear 2 minutes. Transfer to a baking dish, roast 10-12 minutes (130-135°F/55-57°C).
3. Mix melted butter, garlic, and thyme, brush over the duck, and rest 5 minutes.
4. Meanwhile, sauté green beans in butter with garlic powder, salt, and pepper for 5-6 minutes.
5. Serve sliced duck with garlic butter sauce and green beans.

Nutritional Facts (Per Serving): Calories: 580 | Sugars: 1g | Fat: 46g | Carbohydrates: 5g | Protein: 40g | Fiber: 5g | Sodium: 490 mg

CHAPTER 20: BONUSES

30-Day Meal Plans with Shopping Guides: Simplified Keto Planning Made Easy

This cookbook includes a convenient 30-day shopping list tailored to the recipes within, designed to serve one person. The list emphasizes wholesome, high-quality ingredients that align with ketogenic principles, focusing on healthy fats, low carbs, and avoiding overly processed foods. Pay attention to hidden carbs in condiments and feel free to adjust quantities to suit your personal preferences. Dive into effortless, delicious keto cooking and make your journey to better health enjoyable and stress-free!

Grocery Shopping List for 7-Day Meal Plan

- **Meat & Poultry:**
- Chicken breast (boneless, skinless) – 2 lb / 900 g (Mediterranean Chicken & Vegetable Skewers, Zesty Lemon Herb Chicken Wings)
- Ground turkey – 1 lb / 450 g (Mediterranean Roasted Vegetables with Turkey & Feta Power Bowl)
- Chicken thighs – 1 lb / 450 g (Keto Chicken Piccata with Zoodles)
- Shrimp (peeled and deveined) – 12 oz / 340 g (Herb Butter Shrimp with Creamy Cauliflower Gruyère Mash)
- Bacon – 6 oz / 170 g (Pesto Mushroom & Sundried Tomato Bacon Bake)
- Beef (lean) – 1 lb / 450 g (Savory Beef Hash with Butternut Squash and Bell Peppers)
- Fish & Seafood:
- Salmon fillets – 2 lb / 900 g (Pesto-Crusted Salmon with Red Cabbage and Kale Salad)
- Cod fillets – 12 oz / 340 g (Baked Cod with Olive Tapenade & Roasted Cherry Tomatoes)
- Sardines (optional for variation) – 2 cans (Mediterranean-style dishes)

- **Vegetables:**
- Spinach (fresh) – 4 bunches (Greek-Style Egg Bake with Feta, Spinach, and Kalamata Olives, Mediterranean Chicken & Vegetable Skewers)
- Kale – 2 bunches (Slow-Cooked Lemon Herb Chicken & Kale Soup, Mediterranean Eggplant & Tomato Stew)
- Zucchini – 3 large (Keto Chicken Piccata with Zoodles, Mediterranean Roasted Vegetables)
- Cauliflower – 1 large head (Spanish-Inspired Seafood Medley with Saffron Cauliflower Rice, Herb Butter Shrimp with Creamy Cauliflower Gruyère Mash)
- Broccoli – 2 bunches (Beef & Broccoli Keto Stir-Fry with Sesame Oil and Vegetables)
- Eggplant – 2 large (Mediterranean Eggplant & Tomato Stew)
- Red bell peppers – 4 medium (Mediterranean Chicken & Vegetable Skewers, Mediterranean Roasted Vegetables)
- Garlic – 2 bulbs (Various recipes)
- Tomatoes – 8 medium (Mediterranean Eggplant & Tomato Stew, Mediterranean Roasted Vegetables, Keto Beef Wellington)

- Fresh basil – 1 bunch (Mediterranean Eggplant & Tomato Stew, Grilled Chicken Caesar Salad)
- Asparagus – 1 bunch (Herb Butter Shrimp with Creamy Cauliflower Gruyère Mash)
- **Fruits**:
- Lemons – 6 medium (Zesty Lemon Herb Chicken Wings, Pesto Mushroom & Sundried Tomato Bacon Bake, Keto Chicken Piccata)
- Avocados – 4 large (Pesto-Crusted Salmon, Coconut & Chia Keto Breakfast Pudding)
- Berries (mixed, fresh or frozen) – 1 pint / 300 g (Spiced Berry Crumble "Bonfai Toffee" with Almond Flour Crust)
- Dairy & Eggs:
- Feta cheese – 8 oz / 225 g (Greek-Style Egg Bake with Feta, Spinach, and Kalamata Olives)
- Parmesan cheese – 6 oz / 170 g (Keto Chicken Piccata with Zoodles, Grilled Chicken Caesar Salad)
- Mozzarella cheese – 8 oz / 225 g (Pesto-Crusted Salmon with Red Cabbage and Kale Salad)
- Halloumi cheese – 8 oz / 225 g (Grilled Chicken Caesar Salad)
- Cream cheese (full-fat) – 8 oz / 225 g (Sugar-Free Walnut & Dark Chocolate Cream Cheese Truffles)
- Heavy cream – 1 pint / 500 ml (Various recipes)

Grocery Shopping List for 8-14 Day Meal Plan

- **Meat & Poultry:**
- Chicken breast (boneless, skinless) – 2 lb / 900 g (Keto Chicken and Spinach Creamy Risotto, Keto Chicken Fajita Lettuce Wraps)
- Ground turkey – 1 lb / 450 g (Savory Mushroom & Sage Ground Turkey Stew)
- Ground beef (lean) – 1 lb / 450 g (Beef Minced, Spinach & Cheddar Savory Waffle Sandwiches, Keto Beef Wellington)
- Pork chops (boneless) – 2 lb / 900 g (Keto Pork and Pistachio Meat Fingers)
- Bacon – 6 oz / 170 g (Bacon and Broccoli Keto Risotto)
- Shrimp (peeled and deveined) – 12 oz / 340 g (Herb Butter Shrimp with Creamy Cauliflower Gruyère Mash)
- Fish & Seafood:
- Mackerel fillets – 2 lb / 900 g (Grilled Mackerel with Caper & Lemon Dressing)
- Salmon fillets – 12 oz / 340 g (Avocado & Smoked Salmon Breakfast Boats)
- Cod fillets – 12 oz / 340 g (Baked Cod for other recipes, optional)
- **Vegetables:**
- Spinach (fresh) – 4 bunches (Keto Chicken and Spinach Creamy Risotto, Slow-Cooked Chicken and Artichoke Stew, Grilled Chicken Caesar Salad)
- Broccoli – 2 bunches (Bacon and Broccoli Keto Risotto, Cheesy Broccoli & Ham Egg Cups)
- Zucchini – 3 large (Cheddar & Zucchini Herb Muffins with Thyme and Chives, Beef Minced Savory Waffle Sandwiches)
- Cauliflower – 1 head (Creamy Cauliflower Gruyère Mash, Keto Beef Wellington)
- Bell peppers – 4 medium (Mushroom & Feta Stuffed Bell Peppers, Greek-Inspired Stuffed Bell Pepper Halves)
- Garlic – 2 bulbs (Various recipes)
- Tomatoes – 6 medium (Greek-Inspired Stuffed Bell Pepper Halves)
- Lemon – 3 medium (Grilled Mackerel with Caper & Lemon Dressing, Keto Chicken Fajita Lettuce Wraps)
- Fresh herbs (rosemary, thyme, sage) – 1 bunch each (Savory Mushroom & Sage Ground Turkey Stew, Cheddar & Zucchini Herb Muffins)
- Cucumber – 2 medium (Grilled Chicken Caesar Salad, Pesto Parmesan Dip)
- Mushrooms – 8 oz / 225 g (Mushroom & Feta Stuffed Bell Peppers, Herb Butter Shrimp with Creamy Cauliflower Gruyère Mash)
- Avocados – 4 large (Avocado & Smoked Salmon Breakfast Boats, Guacamole for Keto Fajitas)
- Red onion – 1 medium (Keto Chicken Fajita Lettuce Wraps)
- **Fruits:**
- Berries (mixed, fresh or frozen) – 1 pint / 300 g (Vanilla Chia Seed Breakfast Pudding, Keto Chocolate Ganache Tart)
- Lemons – 6 medium (Various recipes)
- **Dairy & Eggs:**
- Feta cheese – 8 oz / 225 g (Mushroom & Feta Stuffed Bell Peppers, Mediterranean Roasted Vegetables with Turkey & Feta Power Bowl)
- Parmesan cheese – 6 oz / 170 g (Keto Pesto Parmesan Dip, Grilled Chicken Caesar Salad with Parmesan Crisps)
- Mozzarella cheese – 8 oz / 225 g (Keto Beef Wellington)
- Cheddar cheese – 6 oz / 170 g (Cheddar & Zucchini Herb Muffins with Thyme and Chives, Beef Minced Savory Waffle Sandwiches)
- Halloumi cheese – 8 oz / 225 g (Grilled Halloumi Salad)
- Greek yogurt (plain, full-fat) – 2 cups / 500 g (Greek Yogurt Parfait, Tzatziki Sauce)
- Eggs – 18 large (Various recipes)
- Cream cheese – 8 oz / 225 g (Keto Vanilla Bean Panna Cotta, Keto Chocolate Ganache Tart)
- Greek yogurt (plain, full-fat) – 2 cups / 500 g (Pesto-Crusted Salmon, Zesty Lemon Herb Chicken Wings)
- **Nuts & Seeds:**
- Almond flour – 1 cup / 120 g (Spiced Berry Crumble "Bonfai Toffee" with Almond Flour Crust, Keto Beef Wellington)
- Chia seeds – ½ cup / 75 g (Coconut & Chia Keto Breakfast Pudding)
- Walnuts – 1 cup / 150 g (Sugar-Free Walnut & Dark Chocolate Cream Cheese Truffles)
- **Pantry Staples:**
- Olive oil (extra virgin) – 1 bottle (Various recipes)
- Coconut oil – 1 jar (Pesto Mushroom & Sundried Tomato Bacon Bake)
- Tzatziki sauce – 1 jar or make fresh (Mediterranean Chicken & Vegetable Skewers)
- Balsamic vinegar – 1 small bottle (Mediterranean Roasted Vegetables)
- Saffron – a pinch (Spanish-Inspired Seafood Medley with Saffron Cauliflower Rice)
- Tahini – 1 jar (Mediterranean Roasted Vegetables with Turkey & Feta Power Bowl)
- Apple cider vinegar – 1 small bottle (Various recipes)
- Cumin powder – 1 small jar (Various recipes)
- Paprika – 1 small jar (Beef & Broccoli Keto Stir-Fry)
- Sesame oil – 1 bottle (Beef & Broccoli Keto Stir-Fry with Sesame Oil)
- Almond milk (unsweetened) – 1 carton (Creamy Avocado Cilantro Lime Dip)
- Spices & Herbs:
- Dried oregano – 1 small jar (Mediterranean Chicken & Vegetable Skewers)
- Dried thyme – 1 small jar (Keto Chicken Piccata with Zoodles)
- Black pepper – 1 small jar (Various recipes)
- Sea salt – 1 small jar (Various recipes)

- Heavy cream – 1 pint / 500 ml (Keto Chicken and Spinach Creamy Risotto, Keto Beef Wellington)
- **Nuts & Seeds:**
- Almond flour – 1 cup / 120 g (Keto Almond Butter Cookies, Beef Minced Savory Waffle Sandwiches)
- Chia seeds – ½ cup / 75 g (Vanilla Chia Seed Breakfast Pudding)
- Pine nuts – ½ cup / 75 g (Keto Pesto Parmesan Dip)
- Walnuts – 1 cup / 150 g (Keto Almond Butter Cookies, Keto Chocolate Ganache Tart)
- Pantry Staples:
- Olive oil (extra virgin) – 1 bottle (Various recipes)
- Coconut oil – 1 jar (Pesto Mushroom & Sundried Tomato Bacon Bake, Stir-Fries)
- Apple cider vinegar – 1 bottle (Various recipes)
- Tahini – 1 jar (Mediterranean Roasted Vegetables with Turkey & Feta Power Bowl, Roasted Red Pepper Hummus)
- Balsamic vinegar – 1 small bottle (Mediterranean Roasted Vegetables, Salads)
- Sesame oil – 1 bottle (Beef & Broccoli Keto Stir-Fry, Zucchini Fritters)
- Almond milk (unsweetened) – 1 carton (Keto Smoothies, Keto Pancakes)
- Spices & Herbs:
- Black pepper – 1 small jar (Various recipes)
- Sea salt – 1 small jar (Various recipes)
- Oregano (dried) – 1 small jar (Greek Salad, Mediterranean Skewers)
- Rosemary (fresh) – 1 bunch (Roasted Chicken, Herb-Crusted Pork Chops)

Grocery Shopping List for 15-21 Day Meal Plan

Meat & Poultry:
Chicken thighs (bone-in or boneless) – 2 lb / 900 g (Keto BBQ Chicken Thighs with Apple Cabbage Slaw, Slow-Cooked Lemon Herb Chicken & Kale Soup)
Ground beef (lean) – 1 lb / 450 g (Keto Bacon Cheeseburger Soup)
Shrimp (peeled and deveined) – 12 oz / 340 g (Herb Butter Shrimp with Creamy Cauliflower Gruyère Mash)
Pork bacon – 6 oz / 170 g (Keto Bacon Cheeseburger Soup, Keto Cheese Boats with Egg and Tomatoes)
Beef tenderloin – 1 lb / 450 g (Keto Beef Wellington)
Salmon fillets – 2 lb / 900 g (Pesto-Crusted Salmon with Red Cabbage and Kale Salad, Spanish-Inspired Seafood Medley with Saffron Cauliflower Rice)
Mackerel fillets – 2 lb / 900 g (Grilled Mackerel with Caper & Lemon Dressing, Spanish-Inspired Seafood Medley with Saffron Cauliflower Rice)
Fish & Seafood:
Cod fillets – 12 oz / 340 g (Baked Cod with Olive Tapenade & Roasted Cherry Tomatoes)
Sardines (optional for variation) – 2 cans (Mediterranean-style dishes)
Vegetables:
Spinach (fresh) – 3 bunches (Keto Egg Bowl with Ginger and Scallions, Mediterranean Eggplant & Tomato Stew)
Broccoli – 2 bunches (Keto Broccoli Waffles with Spicy Yogurt Dip, Beef & Broccoli Keto Stir-Fry with Sesame Oil)
Zucchini – 3 large (Keto Cheese Boats with Egg and Tomatoes, Cheesy Zucchini & Herb Breakfast Casserole)
Cauliflower – 2 heads (Creamy Cauliflower Gruyère Mash, Roasted Cauliflower & Red Pepper Stew)
Tomatoes – 10 medium (Keto Cheese Boats with Egg and Tomatoes, Roasted Cherry Tomatoes)
Kale – 2 bunches (Kale Salad with Lemon Dressing, Keto Chicken and Spinach Creamy Risotto)
Eggplant – 2 large (Mediterranean Eggplant & Tomato Stew)
Bell peppers – 4 medium (Mediterranean Eggplant & Tomato Stew, Roasted Cauliflower & Red Pepper Stew)
Asparagus – 1 bunch (Grilled Mackerel with Caper & Lemon Dressing)
Avocados – 6 large (Keto Egg Bowl, Creamy Avocado Cilantro Lime Dip, Guacamole for Keto Fajitas)
Garlic – 3 bulbs (Various recipes)
Red onion – 1 medium (Keto Beef Wellington, Keto BBQ Chicken Thighs)
Lemons – 6 medium (Grilled Mackerel with Caper & Lemon Dressing, Spicy Avocado Jalapeño Cream Sauce)
Fruits:
Berries (mixed, fresh or frozen) – 2 pints / 600 g (Spiced Berry Crumble "Bonfire Toffee", Keto Berry Coconut Smoothie)
Lemon – 6 medium (Lemon Herb Chicken Wings, Grilled Mackerel with Caper & Lemon Dressing)
Dairy & Eggs:
Feta cheese – 8 oz / 225 g (Mediterranean Roasted Vegetables with Turkey & Feta Power Bowl, Mediterranean Eggplant & Tomato Stew)
Parmesan cheese – 6 oz / 170 g (Keto Pesto Parmesan Dip, Grilled Chicken Caesar Salad with Parmesan Crisps)
Mozzarella cheese – 8 oz / 225 g (Keto Beef Wellington, Keto Cheese Boats)
Halloumi cheese – 8 oz / 225 g (Grilled Halloumi, Mediterranean Salad)
Cream cheese – 8 oz / 225 g (Keto Vanilla Bean Panna Cotta, Keto Chocolate Ganache Tart)
Greek yogurt (plain, full-fat) – 2 cups / 500 g (Keto Pesto Parmesan Dip, Tzatziki Sauce)
Eggs – 18 large (Various recipes)
Heavy cream – 1 pint / 500 ml (Keto Chicken and Spinach Creamy Risotto, Keto Beef Wellington)
Nuts & Seeds:
Almond flour – 1 cup / 120 g (Keto Almond Butter Cookies, Beef Minced Savory Waffle Sandwiches)
Chia seeds – ½ cup / 75 g (Vanilla Chia Seed Breakfast Pudding, Keto Coconut & Chia Keto Breakfast Pudding)
Pine nuts – ½ cup / 75 g (Keto Pesto Parmesan Dip)
Almonds (whole or chopped) – 1

cup / 150 g (Keto Almond Butter Cookies, Keto Smoothies)

Pantry Staples:
Olive oil (extra virgin) – 1 bottle (Various recipes)
Coconut oil – 1 jar (Pesto Mushroom & Sundried Tomato Bacon Bake, Stir-Fries)
Apple cider vinegar – 1 bottle (Various recipes)
Tahini – 1 jar (Mediterranean Roasted Vegetables with Turkey & Feta Power Bowl, Roasted Red Pepper Hummus)
Balsamic vinegar – 1 bottle (Mediterranean Roasted Vegetables, Salads)
Sesame oil – 1 bottle (Beef & Broccoli Keto Stir-Fry, Zucchini Fritters)
Almond milk (unsweetened) – 1 carton (Keto Smoothies, Keto Pancakes)

Spices & Herbs:
Black pepper – 1 small jar (Various recipes)
Sea salt – 1 small jar (Various recipes)
Oregano (dried) – 1 small jar (Greek Salad, Mediterranean Skewers)
Rosemary (fresh) – 1 bunch (Roasted Chicken, Herb-Crusted Pork Chops)
Cumin – 1 small jar (Various recipes)
Paprika – 1 small jar (Beef & Broccoli Keto Stir-Fry, Zucchini Fritters)
Cinnamon – 1 small jar (Keto Vanilla Bean Panna Cotta)

Grocery Shopping List for 22-30 Day Meal Plan

- **Meat & Poultry:**
- Chicken breast (boneless, skinless) – 2 lb / 900 g (Grilled Chicken Caesar Salad, Keto Chicken Piccata with Zoodles)
- Ground turkey – 1 lb / 450 g (Savory Mushroom & Sage Ground Turkey Stew)
- Ground beef (lean) – 1 lb / 450 g (Bacon Cheeseburger Soup, Keto Beef Wellington)
- Pork (boneless) – 1 lb / 450 g (Keto Pork and Pistachio Meat Fingers)
- Lamb (grilled or chops) – 1 lb / 450 g (Greek Salad with Grilled Lamb)
- Shrimp (peeled and deveined) – 12 oz / 340 g (Herb Butter Shrimp with Creamy Cauliflower Gruyère Mash)
- Mackerel fillets – 2 lb / 900 g (Grilled Mackerel with Caper & Lemon Dressing, Spanish-Inspired Seafood Medley)
- **Fish & Seafood:**
- Cod fillets – 12 oz / 340 g (Baked Cod with Olive Tapenade & Roasted Cherry Tomatoes)
- Sardines (optional for variation) – 2 cans (Mediterranean-style dishes)
- **Vegetables:**
- Spinach (fresh) – 4 bunches (Keto Chicken and Spinach Creamy Risotto, Mediterranean Roasted Vegetables with Turkey & Feta Power Bowl)
- Zucchini – 4 large (Cheddar & Zucchini Herb Muffins with Thyme and Chives, Keto Chicken Piccata with Zoodles)
- Cauliflower – 2 heads (Creamy Cauliflower Gruyère Mash, Roasted Cauliflower & Red Pepper Stew)
- Broccoli – 2 bunches (Cheesy Broccoli & Ham Egg Cups, Beef & Broccoli Keto Stir-Fry with Sesame Oil)
- Tomatoes – 8 medium (Keto Beef Wellington, Roasted Cherry Tomatoes)
- Avocados – 6 large (Avocado & Smoked Salmon Breakfast Boats, Guacamole, Keto Egg Bowl)
- Mushrooms – 12 oz / 340 g (Mushroom & Thyme Crustless Quiche, Herb Butter Shrimp with Creamy Cauliflower Gruyère Mash)
- Red onion – 2 medium (Mediterranean Roasted Vegetables with Turkey & Feta Power Bowl, Keto Beef Wellington)
- Kale – 2 bunches (Kale Salad, Keto Chicken and Spinach Creamy Risotto)
- Cucumber – 2 medium (Grilled Chicken Caesar Salad, Pesto Parmesan Dip)
- Bell peppers – 4 medium (Mediterranean Roasted Vegetables, Roasted Cauliflower & Red Pepper Stew)
- Lemons – 6 medium (Grilled Mackerel with Caper & Lemon Dressing, Keto Chicken Piccata)
- Fresh basil – 1 bunch (Keto Pesto Parmesan Dip, Mediterranean Roasted Vegetables)
- Fresh thyme – 1 bunch (Cheddar & Zucchini Herb Muffins, Mushroom & Goat Cheese Breakfast Skillet)
- Garlic – 3 bulbs (Various recipes)
- **Fruits:**
- Berries (mixed, fresh or frozen) – 2 pints / 600 g (Spiced Berry Crumble "Bonfire Toffee," Keto Berry Coconut Smoothie)
- Lemon – 6 medium (Various recipes)
- **Dairy & Eggs:**
- Feta cheese – 8 oz / 225 g (Mediterranean Roasted Vegetables with Turkey & Feta Power Bowl, Greek Salad with Grilled Lamb)
- Parmesan cheese – 6 oz / 170 g (Grilled Chicken Caesar Salad with Parmesan Crisps, Keto Beef Wellington)
- Mozzarella cheese – 8 oz / 225 g (Keto Beef Wellington, Mushroom & Goat Cheese Breakfast Skillet)
- Cream cheese – 8 oz / 225 g (Keto Vanilla Bean Panna Cotta, Keto Tiramisu)
- Greek yogurt (plain, full-fat) – 2 cups / 500 g (Keto Pesto Parmesan Dip, Tzatziki Sauce)
- Heavy cream – 1 pint / 500 ml (Keto Chicken and Spinach Creamy Risotto, Keto Tiramisu)
- Eggs – 18 large (Various recipes)
- Goat cheese – 6 oz / 170 g (Mushroom & Goat Cheese Breakfast Skillet)
- Nuts & Seeds:
- Almond flour – 1 cup / 120 g (Keto Almond Butter Cookies, Keto Chocolate Ganache Tart)
- Chia seeds – ½ cup / 75 g (Vanilla Chia Seed Breakfast Pudding, Keto Coconut & Chia

- Keto Breakfast Pudding)
- Pine nuts – ½ cup / 75 g (Keto Pesto Parmesan Dip)
- Almonds (whole or chopped) – 1 cup / 150 g (Keto Almond Butter Cookies, Keto Smoothies)
- Pantry Staples:
- Olive oil (extra virgin) – 1 bottle (Various recipes)
- Coconut oil – 1 jar (Pesto Mushroom & Sundried Tomato Bacon Bake, Stir-Fries)
- Apple cider vinegar – 1 bottle (Various recipes)
- Tahini – 1 jar (Mediterranean Roasted Vegetables with Turkey & Feta Power Bowl, Roasted Red Pepper Hummus)
- Balsamic vinegar – 1 small bottle (Mediterranean Roasted Vegetables, Salads)
- Sesame oil – 1 bottle (Beef & Broccoli Keto Stir-Fry, Zucchini Fritters)
- Almond milk (unsweetened) – 1 carton (Keto Smoothies, Keto Pancakes)
- Spices & Herbs:
- Black pepper – 1 small jar (Various recipes)
- Sea salt – 1 small jar (Various recipes)
- Oregano (dried) – 1 small jar (Greek Salad, Mediterranean Skewers)
- Rosemary (fresh) – 1 bunch (Roasted Chicken, Herb-Crusted Pork Chops)
- Cumin – 1 small jar (Various recipes)
- Paprika – 1 small jar (Beef & Broccoli Keto Stir-Fry, Zucchini Fritters)
- Cinnamon – 1 small jar (Keto Vanilla Bean Panna Cotta)

Your Feedback is Valuable!

I hope *Keto Diet Cookbook for Beginners* has made your journey to healthier eating easier and more enjoyable. Every recipe was created to help you prepare quick, delicious, and keto-friendly meals without stress.

Now, I'd love to hear from you! Your feedback not only helps me improve future cookbooks but also assists others who are looking for practical, low-carb, and high-fat meal ideas that support a keto lifestyle.

Why Your Review Matters:

- It helps others decide if this book is the right fit for them.
- It inspires me to keep creating helpful and easy-to-follow keto recipes.
- Your insights shape future books to better meet your needs.

What You Can Share:

- Did the recipes fit well into your daily keto routine?
- Were the instructions simple and easy to follow?
- Has this book helped you embrace the keto lifestyle more easily?

A Small Gesture, A Big Difference

If you've found this book helpful, please take a moment to leave a review on Amazon. Even a few words can help others who are looking for guidance in adopting and maintaining a keto diet.

Thank you for being part of this journey—your support truly makes a difference!

With gratitude,
Emory Stout

Printed in Great Britain
by Amazon